CONVERSATION BETWEEN THE SHULAMITE AND THE KING

31 Days of Intimacy

Neisha-Ann Thompson, PhD

Unless otherwise indicated, the Scriptures quoted are from the New King James Version (NKJV) of the Bible.

Other translations cited include:

AMP – Amplified Bible
KJV – King James Version
MSG – The Message
NIV – New International Version
TPT – The Passion Translation

Copyright © 2021 by Dr. Neisha-Ann Thompson

All rights reserved. This book or any portion thereof may not be reproduced or used in any manner whatsoever, without the express written permission of the publisher, except for the use of brief quotations in a book review.

Printed in the United States of America

ISBN: 9798531205896

Dedication

*I dedicate this book to The One, True Love of my life – my Dôdî. I shudder to think of where I would be without You, my Sweet Companion, my Divine Soul Mate, my Bridegroom-King.
No one else knows the places You've walked with me and the things You've brought me through.
Papa, I owe You my life.
All of me is completely Yours, forever!*

"Ani L'Dodi V'Dodi Li"

Table of Contents

Dedication iii
Foreword vii
Day 1 - "Let Him" 1
Day 2 - "Yet You Are So Lovely" 5
Day 3 - "Tell Me" 9
Day 4 - "How I See You" 13
Day 5 - "Bundle of Myrrh" 17
Day 6 - "Dôdî" 21
Day 7 - "His Rose" 25
Day 8 - "At Rest" 29
Day 9 - "Come Closer" 33
Day 10 - "Now Is The Time" 37
Day 11 - "A New Day of Destiny" 41
Day 12 - "The Little Foxes" 45
Day 13 - "Another Time" 49
Day 14 - "I Must Rise" 53
Day 15 - "I Found The One" 57
Day 16 - "Who Is This One?" 61
Day 17 - "The Mercy Seat" 65
Day 18 - "You Are Beauty Itself" 69
Day 19 - "Inner Strength" 73
Day 20 - "I Will Go" 77
Day 21 - "Now You Are Ready" 81
Day 22 - "Spare Nothing" 85

Day 23 - "Deeper Still" 89
Day 24 - "My Soul Melted" 93
Day 25 - "I Endured All" 97
Day 26 - "None Like Him" 101
Day 27 - "The Favorite One" 105
Day 28 - "Open Hearts" 109
Day 29 - "A Claiming Love" 113
Day 30 - "Unrelenting Fire" 117
Day 31 - "Unquenchable Love" 121
The Bridegroom And The Bride In Divine Duet 125
Prayer 127
Reference 128
About The Author 129

Foreword

The Lord has been speaking to me for a while about finding my identity in His love. I did not quite understand what that meant and so I decided to embark on a journey of discovery, which Holy Spirit led me to start by studying the Book of Song of Solomon. The insight and revelation that I gained left me in tears as I pored over each verse of that beautiful eight-chapter book for months. The love of God so thoroughly engulfed me that Holy Spirit moved me to share His revelations in a 31-Day Devotional.

If you have ever dealt with shame, fear, rejection, neglect, unworthiness, and/or emotional abandonment, it is sometimes hard to accept love, or to even believe that you are worthy of love. When we are loved *conditionally*, conditions of worth are applied to us that cause us to feel like we're only worthy of love if we fulfill the stated conditions or meet the expected requirements. In order to meet those conditions and requirements, we engage in all kinds of acts or practices just to feel loved. When we understand that we are *unconditionally* loved by God, however, it frees us from the striving, performance-based, works-mentality that keeps us in a cycle of feeling like we have to jump through hoops, or be perfect, to be approved and accepted. Working to *earn* the love of another is exhausting and debilitating. God wants to build our identities in *His* love. Not in our qualifications or performance, but purely in His unconditional, no-strings-attached, love.

This 31-Day Devotional will take you deeper into the heart of our Bridegroom-King as we listen more intently to His conversation with His Bride, The Shulamite. Recognize that regardless of your gender, we are all The Shulamite (Bride of Christ) and He is our Bridegroom-King. I pray that you will open up your heart to receive the love He wants to flood you with as you walk these thirty-one days out with Him. The conversations explored are raw and vulnerable – they speak of an unfiltered, passionate love between one who sees "herself" as so unworthy, and One who will stop at nothing to dismantle that ungodly belief.

May Holy Spirit rend and ravish your heart as you embark on this journey into deeper intimacy with our Bridegroom-King!

Day One
"Let Him"

The Shulamite: *Let Him smother me with kisses – His Spirit-kiss divine. So kind are Your caresses, I drink them in like the sweetest wine.*
– Song of Solomon 1:2 TPT

I love how the chapter begins with those two words, *"Let Him."* To *let* simply means to allow. This is so important because no level of intimacy begins with force or pressure. An intimate relationship with God is no different. In order to experience true intimacy with God, we have to yield, submit, and surrender ourselves to His love. It involves a willingness. We have to "Let Him" do what He wants to do to bait us in deeper and to pull us in closer. So, The Shulamite begins the conversation with this realization that intimacy with the King first starts with her willingness to yield to His affection for her.

Has someone ever forced their affection on you before? I can only imagine how uncomfortable and offensive that would feel to you as the unsuspecting party. Our King would never force His love on us in that way. He waits to be invited, to be entreated. *Then*, He proceeds to express His love for us. In Song of Solomon 1:2 TPT, The Shulamite describes The King's caresses and His Spirit-kisses, which are not to be confused with a human caress or kiss. As I studied this verse, I learned in one of the commentaries that the Hebrew word for "kiss" is "nashaq," which means to equip or to arm for battle. As I reflected more on the kiss that literally equips, I thought about how warfare training really begins in intimate fellowship. Oftentimes we focus on the *rigors* of spiritual warfare preparation and we forsake the most important aspect – that strategic warfare tactic that best equips us against our adversary – *intimacy with God*. May we never go to battle without first being kissed by our King.

How can a kiss equip us for battle? I think about the act of kissing and how comforting, encouraging, and affirming it can be. A toddler falls and bruises his knee, and with just one kiss from his mother the pain seems to miraculously go away. I believe that in "letting" our King kiss us, we receive an impenetrable buffer of comfort, encouragement, and affirmation that helps us in the heat of any battle. So, as He kisses us with His Spirit-kiss divine, He is really arming and equipping us for everything we're going to face. If we are unwilling to "Let Him" then we will be ill-equipped as soldiers or warriors in the Army of the Lord. How many lost battles would have been won if we were first *equipped* in intimate fellowship? What other kiss can so boost your confidence, disarm your fears, and cause you to run *to* the battle line with joy? There's no other!

I don't know about you, but it sure helps to know in the midst of the most challenging battle, that I have been *equipped by Love*!

Prayer: *Thank You for Your love, my Bridegroom-King. Yours is a love that bolsters and equips. Today, I open up my heart to receive Your nashaq. I surrender to Your equipping. Yes, I drink in Your kisses and Your caresses like the sweetest wine. Admittedly, I have not always felt worthy of this love – in fact there have been times in my life that I have rejected it. But, here I am, Lord. I'm open and I'm ready to be fully equipped by You as Your Shulamite. Today, I "let" You!*

Conversation With The King

Conversation With The King

_____

_____

_____

_____

_____

_____

_____

_____

_____

_____

_____

_____

_____

_____

_____

_____

_____

Day Two
"Yet You Are So Lovely"

The Shulamite: *Jerusalem Maidens, in this twilight darkness*
I know I am so unworthy
— so in need.
The King: *Yet you are so lovely!*
The Shulamite: *I feel as dark and dry as the desert tents of*
the wandering nomads.
The King: *Yet you are so lovely — like the fine linen tapestry*
hanging in the Holy Place.
- Song of Solomon 1:5 TPT

This particular exchange between The Shulamite and The King reveals so much about how we see ourselves in comparison to how God sees us. I want you to reread the verse, inserting your name where it says [The Shulamite] and imagine the King saying, "*Yet you are so lovely*" to your insistence on all the things you think make you unworthy. Isn't it amazing how we can argue away any semblance of our worth or worthiness? How quick we sometimes are to highlight what we deem as flaws and to use them as disqualifiers? How we can come so fully in agreement with the ungodly belief that we are unworthy *because* of our flaws, that we try to unconsciously convince others of this lie? My friend, The Shulamite is you and me.

I cannot tell you the countless times that I have used my flaws and shortcomings as disqualifiers. Sometimes it is hard to fathom a love that is actually unconditional. As human beings, we *say* we love unconditionally, but this is very rarely the case. *Conditions of worth* are prerequisites that we create to determine whether or not someone is worthy of our love or acceptance. For example, if someone hurts or offends us, we may withhold acceptance or love until *we* determine that their apology is sincere enough, or that they have served sufficient time in the prison of our heart. We apply conditions of worth all the time in our relationships. And when we consider this human way, it is hard for us to accept a Love that has no conditions, no prerequisites, no prison time, and no recollection of past offenses. It sounds quite absurd. Yet, that is the love our King has for us. That is the love He has for you!

There is nothing that you can ever say or do that will disqualify you from God's love. This is the same God who tells us in His Word that nothing shall ever be able to separate us from His love (Romans 8:38-39); not even our own guilty hearts or consciences.

Whenever our hearts make us feel guilty and remind us of our failures, we know that God is much greater and more merciful than our conscience, and He knows everything there is to know about us. - 1 John 3:20 TPT

How amazing it is to be known so fully and yet loved so defiantly! Beloved, you are lovely to The King – flaws, mistakes, shortcomings, wrongdoings, and all – and no excuse you give Him for your misperceived unworthiness will ever suffice. He will always rebut your strongest argument with, *"Yet you are so lovely!"* Because, to Him, you are! That is all He sees when He looks at you. *Selah*.

Prayer: *Thank You for Your love, my Bridegroom-King. Yours is a love that never relents. It refuses to bow to my insecurities or feelings of low self-worth. It has taken me a while to accept*

this stubborn Love, but I open up my heart to it today. The realization that You respond to all my misperceived disqualifiers with a defiant, "Yet, you are so lovely!" – completely consumes my heart. Help me to see myself the way You see me and to live from that place of secure "knowing."

Conversation With The King

Day Three
"Tell Me"

The Shulamite: *Won't you tell me, Lover of my soul, where do You feed Your flock? Where do You lead Your beloved ones to rest in the heat of the day? Why should I be like a veiled woman as I wander among the flocks of Your shepherds?*
The King: *Listen, My radiant one – if you ever lose sight of Me, just follow in My footsteps where I lead My lovers. Come with your burdens and cares. Come to the place near the sanctuary of My shepherds.*
- Song of Solomon 1:7-8 TPT

Right on the heels of trying to prove her *un*worthiness to The King, The Shulamite now wants to know how she can connect with His fellow lovers. You see, one encounter with the love of God will have you yearning for more and more of Him! She asked the question, *"Why should I be like a veiled woman as I wander among the flocks of Your shepherds?"* In other words, *"Why should I hide my identity? I want to be identified as one of Yours. I want to be fed where You feed Your flock. I want to rest where You lead Your beloved ones to rest."* The Shulamite is coming into her identity. She calls The King, *"Lover of my soul."*

He then responds to her request – *Tell me!* – by inviting her into deeper intimacy and fellowship. *"If you ever lose sight of Me, just follow My footsteps..."* Isn't this true about our everyday walk with God? Once we abide in Him and follow where He leads us – *as* He leads us – He will always be in view. Have you lost sight of Him today? Have the cares of this world and the pressures of this life blinded your eyes to where He is, or where He's leading? If you find yourself feeling lost today, don't despair! The fact that The King starts off by saying, "*If you ever lose sight of Me,*" tells us that it is quite possible to be His lover and yet lose sight of Him at times. Don't beat yourself up if you have lost sight of Him. We all have at one point or another in this Christian walk. Remember, The King is never angry at you. When Jesus Christ died on the cross, He took all the wrath of God on Himself. You will never, ever experience the wrath of God (John 5:24). Rest in that Truth today.

So, how do we follow in The King's footsteps? We do this by daily spending time in His presence in prayer, worship, and reading the Word.

Truth's shining light guides me in my choices and decisions; the revelation of Your Word makes my pathway clear.
- Psalm 119:105 TPT

He invites us to come with our burdens and cares; to come to the place near the sanctuary of His shepherds. That word *sanctuary* means a place of refuge or safety. It is there that He invites us to come with all the things that weigh us down and burden our hearts. He invites us to follow His footsteps to that place. Will you follow Him there today? Will you spend some time in His presence and watch Him lead you into that place of refuge and safety, prepared and reserved for all His lovers? He's waiting patiently for you.

Prayer: *O my Bridegroom-King, I'm so tired! So exhausted! The pressures and cares of this life have weighed me down and have caused me at times to lose sight of You. Will You please forgive me? I desire to come to the place near the sanctuary of Your shepherds. I desire to be where You feed Your flock. Lead me today by Your footsteps. I cast all my burdens and cares on*

You. I remove the veil of shame and fear – I step into my identity as one of Your beloved ones. Restore me. Refresh me. Never stop "telling me," or leading me, O Lover of my soul!

Conversation With The King

Day Four
"How I See You"

The King: *My dearest one [My darling], let Me tell you how I see you – you are so thrilling to Me. To gaze upon you is like looking at one of Pharaoh's finest horses – a strong, regal steed pulling his royal chariot. Your tender cheeks are beautiful – your earrings and gem-laden necklaces set them ablaze. We will enhance your beauty with golden ornaments studded with silver.*

                              - Song of Solomon 1:9-11 TPT

These three verses are so very important as we consider our identity in Christ. It's not at all about how *we* see ourselves or how *others* see us – all that matters is how our King sees us. His is the only view or perspective that truly matters! In the previous verses of this first chapter of the book of Song of Solomon, the King has listened patiently to The Shulamite tell Him how she sees herself, and all the things that she feels disqualify her from receiving His love. Now, He takes the time to respond to her self-*mis*perceptions and affirm who she is in *His* eyes and how *He* sees her. Let's examine each of His descriptors today.

    You are so thrilling to Me. Did you know that *you* bring The King excitement and pleasure? Yes, you! He is excited to commune with you and to draw close to you. He enjoys your company. He's passionate about you. He takes great pleasure in your very life, whether you feel like you've messed it up or not. Hear and receive Him telling you today just how much *you* thrill His heart!

A strong, regal steed. The King compared The Shulamite to a horse. But, not just any horse – one of Pharaoh's finest horses that pulls his royal chariot. Beloved, your King sees you as strong, regardless of how weak you may feel in this moment. Not only does He see you as strong, but He sees you as the *strongest* and the *finest*. Not only are you strong enough to help guide kings ("pulling Pharaoh's royal chariot"), but you, yourself, are worthy of being part of a royal procession!

While in prayer one day, I had a vision of *Papa* (my intimate name for God) helping me mount a horse and parading me through different towns for everyone to see. As He led the horse I was riding on from town to town, people would stand to the side, smiling and cheering us on. When the vision ended, I asked Him what it meant and He told me that it was a reflection of how proud He was of me and how special I was to Him – that He was willing to show me off to everyone as His beloved daughter. That vision truly warmed my heart. Beloved, your King is proud of you. He loves and adores you, and He wants the whole world to know it!

Your tender cheeks are beautiful. When I hear the phrase "*tender* cheeks," I think of youthfulness; and youthfulness brings with it a sense of vulnerability and honesty. The cheeks reflect our emotions as they move in response to the movement of our mouths (whether smiling or frowning). Your King says to you today: "*The vulnerability and honesty of your emotions – how you bring and express yourself to Me – is beautiful in My sight.*" The King is never turned off by the expression of your feelings. Perhaps there are people in your life who have not responded well to your vulnerability and, as a result, you feel unsafe in expressing your true feelings. There is safety in the presence of The King, Beloved. He calls the vulnerability and honesty of your emotions, *beautiful*. Don't withhold yourself from Him today because of the response you may have received from human beings. Remember, God is not human (Numbers 23:19; John 4:24). *Selah*.

I love how The King ends His expression of love for The Shulamite in these verses. He tells her how He plans to enhance her beauty. She is already so beautiful to Him, but He is forever making His Bride more and more into His image. His desire for you today is to look more like Him – He wants to enhance your beauty. Beautification is a process (Ecclesiastes 3:11) that will continue until the day He comes to take us Home to be with Him (Philippians 1:6). He'll never stop working on and with us. He never gets tired or frustrated. He never gives up. What a faithful Lover we have in our King!

Christ's love makes the Church whole. His words evoke her beauty. Everything He does and says is designed to bring the best out of her, dressing her in dazzling white silk, radiant with holiness.
- Ephesians 5:27 MSG

Prayer: *My King, today I thank You for Your beauty. I call it "Your beauty" because You gave it to me! You made me beautiful and strong. Help me to truly see myself the way You see me and to take my rightful place as royalty. I choose to show You my tender cheeks today. I do not withhold my feelings or emotions from You, regardless of how ugly and uncomfortable they may be. Please continue to work on me as You conform me to Your image. My ultimate desire is to be Your mirror – a pure reflection of You in all I say and do, with the very essence of my being.*

Conversation With The King

Day Five
"Bundle of Myrrh"

The Shulamite: *As The King surrounded me at His table, the sweet fragrance of spikenard awakened the night. A sachet of myrrh is my Lover, like a tied-up bundle of myrrh resting over my heart.*
- Song of Solomon 1:12-13 TPT

Myrrh was one of the gifts the Magi presented to Jesus when they found Him in the manger. Myrrh is often used as an embalming spice, so it speaks of suffering or death. In giving Jesus this gift, the Magi were prophesying His death on the cross thirty-two years later. Our Beloved King proudly wears this myrrh-fragrance which serves as a reminder of His ultimate sacrifice on the Cross of Calvary. Myrrh symbolizes a form of death or self-denial; but it also symbolizes resurrection!

I want you to consider The Shulamite's desperate love for her King as she describes Him as "*a tied-up bundle of myrrh resting over her heart.*" Beloved, we too wear that invisible sachet of myrrh over our hearts every single day. Our King died for us, so daily we die for Him (1 Corinthians 15:31). That is one of the ways that we get to know Him in a deeper and more intimate way – through the fellowship of His sufferings (Philippians 3:10).

Perhaps you find yourself in a season of suffering today. You can't see your way out and you feel like you're about to break under the weight of all you're currently enduring. You may even feel on the verge of giving up. As counterintuitive as this sounds, I want to encourage you today to: *Embrace* the myrrh. There is a level of deep intimacy in God that can only be attained by way of suffering or self-denial. Not that we inflict suffering on ourselves just to say we are lovers of God – but the kind of suffering for righteousness' sake that enters us into fellowship with Him. It's called the *fellowship* of His suffering (Philippians 3:10) – that means we're not going through it by ourselves; He is with us as we embrace the myrrh. In fact, He wears it as one of His fragrant spices. It has now become *fragrant* because it represents resurrection power – our King's triumph over death, hell, and the grave. Yes, we may suffer at times on this Christian journey, but the myrrh we embrace guarantees us the same resurrection and triumph as our King!

If we suffer, we shall also reign with Him….
- 2 Timothy 2:12a KJV

Prayer: *My Bridegroom-King, please teach me how to truly fellowship with You in suffering. To truly carry the sachet of myrrh in my heart. Help me not to despise suffering with You as it only draws my soul closer to You. Teach me how to embrace the myrrh and allow it to drown my heart in the floodwaters of Your love – into deeper intimacy with You. I want to reign with You, so help me to die to myself daily as I become more and more conformed to Your image and likeness. May I wear You like a tied-up bundle of myrrh, forever resting over my heart.*

Conversation With The King

Conversation With The King

Day Six
"Dôdî"

The King: *My darling, you are so lovely! You are beauty itself to Me. Your passionate eyes are like gentle doves.*
The Shulamite: *My Beloved One, both handsome and winsome, You are pleasing beyond words. Our resting place is anointed and flourishing, like a green forest meadow bathed in light.*
- Song of Solomon 1:15-16 TPT

The King continues to dote on The Shulamite, reminding her incessantly of how beautiful she is to Him. Posture your heart to receive Him telling you – as His Shulamite today – that you are beauty itself to Him! Take a moment just to let that Truth sink deep in your heart (John 8:32). Whatever has happened in your life that has caused you to feel everything but beautiful.... whatever mistakes you've made, whatever has been done to you – receive the Truth today that, in the King's eyes, you are beauty itself!

The Shulamite is so overwhelmed by The King's description of her that she responds with mutual doting. She calls him her "Beloved One." That term in Hebrew is the word *Dôdî*, the root word of which means "to boil." So, in calling The King her Beloved One, The Shulamite is expressing how much her love for Him is piping hot! She is saying she is, metaphorically, boiling over with love and passion for Him. Wow! I believe The King longs for us to not only *call* Him our Dôdî, but to *live* like He's our Dôdî – to live piping hot lives of passionate love for Him (Revelation 3:15-16). The kind of lives that attract others to the heat of our Love.

Perhaps the trials of life have cooled your passion for The King. When you first entered this relationship, you were on fire for Him; but as time has gone by, you find your passion is waning. The truth is, once you accept The King as your Beloved One, that "boiling" – even if now just a simmer – will stir again the minute the fire is ignited. Some of the ways we stoke the fire and stir ourselves up are by: praying daily in the Spirit (Jude 20); daily reading and meditating on His Word (2 Timothy 2:15); daily entering into His gates with Thanksgiving and His courts with praise (Psalm 34:1; Psalm 100:4); and daily loving others (1 John 4:8; Matthew 22:37-40).

It's time to stoke the fire!

The Shulamite, fully ignited by love, begins to describe the resting place of The King. She describes it as anointed, flourishing, green (fresh), and bright (pure, warm). That is the place He beckons you into today, Beloved Shulamite. In this reserved resting place with your Dôdî, you receive a fresh anointing that will destroy every yoke of burden or bondage you may be carrying (Isaiah 10:27). You begin to experience flourishing (prosperity, thriving, growth) in areas that perhaps were barren and dry. There's a freshness and newness of life that await you in this reserved place. In His presence, there is purity and warmth – no evil or darkness; no fakeness or dissimulation. Beloved Shulamite, let's enter in today!

There's a private place reserved for the devoted lovers of Yahweh, where they sit near Him and receive the revelation-secrets of His promises.
- Psalm 25:14 TPT

Let this Truth forever settle your heart and settle every matter in your life:

Ani L'Dodi V'Dodi Li: I am my Beloved's and my Beloved is mine!

Prayer: *Dôdî, truly You are everything to me! I long to burn for You in a way that draws others to the heat of our love. Baptize me afresh with the fire of Your love today. I want to boil over for You. Let Your fire consume every dry and barren place in my heart and life. I want to be a "burning one" for You! I surrender my life to You anew today – I recommit to living not only like You are mine, but also like I am Yours. May "Ani L'Dodi V'Dodi Li" be the banner people see hanging over me every time they see me.*

Conversation With The King

Day Seven
"His Rose"

The Shulamite: *I am truly His rose, the very theme of His song. I'm overshadowed by His love, like a lily growing in the valley!*
The King: *Yes, you are My darling companion. You stand out from all the rest. For though the thorns surround you, you remain as pure as a lily, more than all others.*
- Song of Solomon 2:1-2 TPT

The King calls you His rose today, Beloved Shulamite! A rose is one of the most beautiful flowers ever created. To get a fuller understanding of the symbolism of roses, I did a quick study on their meanings based on color. *Red* roses often symbolize love and romance, while *pink* roses tend to symbolize gratitude and admiration. *Orange* roses symbolize passion and excitement, while *yellow* roses symbolize friendship. Finally, *white* roses symbolize purity and a sense of innocence. As The King calls *you* His rose today, recognize that His expression of love encapsulates all the meanings of the different colors of roses... and more! We can never exhaust the depth of The King's love or His expressions of love toward us.

You are the very theme of His song. I encourage you to press in today to hear what song The King is singing over you. The Psalmist David wrote in Psalm 32:7 –

You are my Hiding Place; You shall protect me from trouble; You surround me with songs and shouts of deliverance. Selah.

I think about the effect music has on us and just how much the right song (with the right lyrics) can set the mood and atmosphere. The King is constantly singing the perfect love song over you, Beloved Shulamite. Consider how many times it was the literal song of the Lord that delivered you from heaviness, or the intense pain of past seasons. He never stops singing over you. You are the very theme of His song!

The King calls The Shulamite, His "darling companion" and puts her in a class all by herself. This one who, just a chapter ago, felt inadequate, insufficient, inferior, and unworthy – this is the one The King says "stands out from all the rest." I sense that is a word of encouragement for someone reading this today. You have disqualified yourself and, even in this moment, you feel like you have nothing to offer and that no one will ever truly *see* you or desire you. I want you to hear your Dôḏî telling you today that *you* are His choice; and not just any choice, His *first* choice – you stand out above all others. Rest in that Truth today!

He goes on to tell The Shulamite that He sees and understands the "thorny" situations that she has been involved in. All the ways and times that the cares and pressures of life have tried to stifle and suffocate her. All the times she fell prey to the thorns and gave in to moments of weakness and despair. The King says today, "I see the thorns that surround you and I understand."

For we have a magnificent King-Priest, Jesus Christ, the Son of God, who rose into the Heavenly realm for us, and now sympathizes with us in our frailty. He understands humanity, for as a man, our magnificent King-Priest was tempted in every way just as we are, and conquered sin. So now we draw near freely and boldly to where grace is enthroned, to receive

mercy's kiss and discover the grace we urgently need to strengthen us in our time of weakness.
- Hebrews 4:14b-16 TPT

Not only did The King understand The Shulamite's situation, but He called her an overcomer. Despite being surrounded by thorns, He celebrated the Truth that she maintained her purity through it all. And I hear that for someone reading this today. You have come down really hard on yourself for all the ways you have messed up and failed, but your King still considers you a victor, an overcomer, and more than a conqueror! It's not about how we feel about ourselves, but it's always about how *The King* sees us and what *He* thinks about us. Let's guard our agreement with Him today. Let's not give room to any thought that is contrary to His high thoughts about us.

Prayer: *My King, words fail to describe just how much You mean to me. To know that You call me Your "darling companion" and You set me in a class all by myself, despite all the ways I've messed up, is overwhelming. To know that You make me the theme of Your song and that You sing over me especially in the night season, comforts my heart. In spite of all the thorny situations in my life, You still call me "pure as a lily." O how You love me! I choose to rest in Your perfect love for me today.*

Conversation With The King

Day Eight
"At Rest"

The Shulamite: *His left hand cradles my head while His right hand holds me close. I am at rest in this love.*
The King: *Promise Me, Jerusalem Maidens, by the gentle gazelles and delicate deer, that you'll not disturb My love until she is ready to arise.*
- Song of Solomon 2:6-7 TPT

Today's devotional reading is especially for those walking through seasons of transition, or the unknown. There have been several changes in your life that have left you feeling a sense of lostness and you're wondering what is going on. At times our Loving King leads us in paths we do not understand and cannot figure out in our human wisdom. It's a testing of the heart to see if we will continue to trust Him and to walk on with Him by faith. This is where The Shulamite finds herself; but her conclusion of the matter is where The King calls us to be.

The Shulamite talks about the left hand of The King cradling her head. The left hand of God symbolizes His mysteries – His ways and movement in our lives that we just do not understand. It is His left hand that cradles the head (the mind) of The Shulamite. Her thoughts are flooded by His mysteries – things that are too high and incomprehensible for her (Job 42:3 MSG). If you find yourself today being cradled by the left hand of your King, take heart. You may not understand His ways, but you know He loves you dearly and would never do anything to hurt you as His darling companion. As His left hand cradles your head today, recognize that *His right hand holds you close.*

Even though The Shulamite does not understand the mysteries of her King, she realizes that she is still being held by Him through it all. Don't miss that Truth today. If we only pay attention to what His left hand is doing, we will miss what His right hand is doing. We serve an ambidextrous God. We cannot form opinions or make conclusions based solely on the movement of one hand. This is especially true when going through challenging seasons of transition where nothing around you makes sense. When The Shulamite considers all of this, she decides to settle her heart and rest in The King's love. That's where He wants you to settle as well, Beloved Shulamite. Despite what you may not understand right now, know that His right hand upholds you; and choose to rest in His unfailing love for you.

Do not yield to fear, for I am always near. Never turn your gaze from Me, for I am your Faithful God. I will infuse you with My strength and help you in every situation. I will hold you firmly with My victorious right hand.
- Isaiah 41:10 TPT

As The Shulamite made the conscious decision to rest in The King's love, He pleaded with the Jerusalem Maidens (friends of The Shulamite) to promise Him that they would not disturb her in this rest. That they would not cause any distractions or remind her of the cares that she'd been carrying. That they would not incite her into trying to figure out The King's ways or His mysteries. Perhaps you have some "Jerusalem Maidens" in your own life who need to make The King this promise today. I've learned that constantly talking to people about "left-hand situations" we do not understand, only leads to more confusion and distress. The King's message to you and all those you're in relationship with today is – *Rest*.

Prayer: *My King, please help me to find and take rest in Your love, even when my mind is being cradled by Your mysteries and the great unknown. Let me not be distracted or distressed by what I do not understand. Please let Your love be my resting place in this season and for the rest of my life. Cause nothing and no one to disturb or awaken me from this rest. Thank You for continuing to hold me with Your right hand through it all. I know that You will never let me go.*

Conversation With The King

Day Nine
"Come Closer"

The Shulamite: *Listen! I hear my Lover's voice. I know it's Him coming to me – leaping with joy over mountains, skipping in love over the hills that separate us, to come to me. Let me describe Him: He is graceful as a gazelle, swift as a wild stag. Now He comes closer, even to the places where I hide. He gazes into my soul, peering through the portal as He blossoms within my heart.*
- Song of Solomon 2:8-9 TPT

The Shulamite is so in tune with The King that she senses His presence from a distance. She hears His voice and she knows He's coming to her. I want to encourage you today, regardless of where you may find yourself, The King is coming to you. He leaps with joy over mountains and skips in love over the hills that may be separating you from Him in this moment.

There's no shadow He won't light up
Mountain He won't climb up
Coming after you
There's no wall He won't kick down
Lie He won't tear down
Coming after you
(Asbury, 2018, Track 1)

The distance does not stop Him from coming to where you are right now. He takes pleasure in climbing over mountains and hills just to get to you. You are never out of His reach and you are never alone. May this Truth settle your heart today.

Not only does The King draw closer to The Shulamite – as He's drawing close to you in this moment – but He comes *even closer* to the places where she hides. Beloved Shulamite, your King is neither intimidated nor turned off by the things that drive you into hiding. Because He is omniscient, there is nothing that He does not know. And because He knows all things, He knew everything that you would ever do and He has taken all your mistakes into account, as He has so beautifully planned out your life! He's not afraid of *where* you hide or *what* you have to hide. Nothing about you repulses or offends Him. He comes closer to you today.

The Shulamite describes The King "*gazing into her soul, peering through the portal…*" Now, that's true intimacy! Knowing that you are fully seen and fully known, yet fully loved. Being willing to allow the Lover of your soul to come closer to the places in your heart and life that you have been afraid to open up and show to anyone. Or that perhaps you tried showing to others, but were rejected as a result. He longs to rush into those places today. The places where we've carried shame and guilt – where we've disqualified ourselves from ever being truly seen and truly loved. Beloved Shulamite, embrace the warmth of His gaze today. His is not the cold, piercing stare that many of us have become accustomed to when people see our flaws; His is a look of love, mercy, compassion, and unconditional acceptance.

It's interesting that up until this point, The King is referred to in the Book of Song of Solomon as *The Shepherd-King*. But, after The Shulamite realizes how much He wants to come closer to her, He is later referred to as *The Bridegroom-King*. It was the level of intimacy and vulnerability that came from Him coming close to her hiding places, that marked the transition from Shepherd to Bridegroom. We can only be so intimate with The Shepherd. A deeper level of intimacy – the nakedness of vulnerability – requires relationship with The Bridegroom. This relationship involves a *drawing in*, a *leading out*, and the *abandoning of the familiar*. That's the level of intimate fellowship The King wants to have with you. Will you allow Him to come closer today?

Prayer: *My heart feels truly ravished by Your desire to enter my hiding places, my Bridegroom-King. For so long I have felt afraid to let anyone in because of how people have handled my flaws in the past. Calvary drew You closer to me and yet, today, You draw closer still. I invite You in. Just as You invited Your disciple Thomas to touch Your wounds, I invite You today to touch mine. Gaze into my soul, O Bridegroom-King. Draw me in, lead me out, and cause me to abandon my familiar hiding places for the wide, open spaces You have prepared and reserved for me. Come closer today. I let You in.*

Conversation With The King

Day Ten
"Now Is The Time"

The King: *The one I love calls to Me: Arise My dearest. Hurry, My darling. Come away with Me! I have come as you have asked, to draw you to My heart and lead you out. For now is the time, My beautiful one.*
- Song of Solomon 2:10 TPT

Yesterday we explored the idea that The Shulamite *sensed* her King coming closer to her – skipping over mountains and hills to get to her. Today, we read that she was right! The King was, in fact, on His way to her and now invites her to "come away" with Him. At different points in your walk with God, you will sense His invitation to come away with Him. I describe it as a "summoning" into His presence; where you suddenly feel so overwhelmed by His love that you drop everything and find a quiet place to engage Him. If you've never experienced His summoning, He's beckoning you today to come away with Him.

The world we live in is filled with so many distractions. So many things tug at our hearts and attempt to redirect our gaze from our King. It's a literal fight to stay focused on the Lord and to keep your heart fixed on Him. The heart is truly an idol factory. It creates new idols every day, out of any and everything. It's never about whether or not we have idols but, rather, which idol is vying for the throne of our hearts at any given moment. This is why The King constantly invites us to come away with Him. He knows how easily our human hearts can get distracted by lesser loves. Today, He has not only come to draw you to His heart, but He has come to lead you out!

The King has come to lead you out of everything that has held you captive. He's come to lead you out of all the places where you have been preoccupied with distractors and distractions. There are seasons where He chooses to join us in those places as we struggle to break free; but then there is the appointed time for our complete deliverance and freedom. The invitation today is not a *joining in*, but a *drawing out*.

He reached down from on high and took hold of me; He drew me out of deep waters.
- Psalm 18:16 NIV

I want you to pause for a moment and just ask The King what has been distracting you from His presence in this season of your life. Perhaps you can write His answer on the journal page that follows today's devotional reading. What is it that has competed with Him for your attention? What is it in your life that makes the invitation to come away with Him hard to accept? What idol in your life is God's biggest rival today? Is it money? A relationship? A person? A title? A dream?

Confess that to The King in this moment and invite Him to draw you to His heart and lead you out of these places. Some of us have been in bondage for a while, always coming up with an excuse as to why we can't abandon everything for the secret place of prayer. While our King continues to be patient and long-suffering with us, I hear Him saying today – *"Now is the time."* Let's not delay.

Prayer: *My Bridegroom-King, I respond to Your invitation to come away with You today. Please forgive me for the many times I've ignored You because of life's distractions. I confess every distractor and every idol, and I repent in Your presence.*

Please refocus and realign me. Draw me to Your heart and lead me out of the distracting places I've dwelt in. My desire is to come away with You – to abandon everything, at any time, to be with You. Help me set my heart today. Help me fix my gaze. I make no more excuses and I will not delay any longer. I agree with You that now is the time and my answer today is, "Yes!"

Conversation With The King

Day Eleven
"A New Day of Destiny"

The King: *The season has changed, the bondage of your barren winter has ended, and the season of hiding is over and gone. The rains have soaked the earth and left it bright with blossoming flowers. The season for singing and pruning the vines has arrived. I hear the cooing of the doves in our land, filling the air with songs to awaken you and guide you forth. Can you not discern this new day of destiny breaking forth around you? The early signs of My purposes and plans are bursting forth...*
- Song of Solomon 2:11-13a TPT

I declare over you today that this is a new day of destiny! The season has changed and the early signs of God's purposes and plans for your life are bursting forth even now! Receive the Word of the Lord to you today, in Jesus Name!

You have gone through a long, hard season of barren winter. It has felt like nothing has flourished, blossomed, or bloomed in your life in this past season. In fact, you may have felt at times like you missed God, or you were in the wrong place at the wrong time. Perhaps you went into hiding as a result of feeling like God was not pleased with you, or like you messed up too badly to ever face Him again. If you have felt or thought any of these things, I want to encourage you today that God has not taken His eyes off you, nor has He removed His hand from your life. I hear the cooing of doves in your land! The cooing of doves only happens at harvest time, so the sound signifies that your harvest season is here, Beloved Shulamite!

Those who sow their tears as seeds will reap a harvest with joyful shouts of glee. They may weep as they go out carrying their seed to sow, but they will return with joyful laughter and shouting with gladness as they bring back armloads of blessing and a harvest overflowing!
- Psalm 126:5-6 TPT

The world has just endured one of the hardest seasons in history, where we have been stretched and tried beyond anything we could have ever imagined. In many ways, we were stripped of personal freedoms that we previously enjoyed; and were forced to make hard decisions that sometimes held devastating consequences. But, hear your King proclaiming over you today that this storm that you have just come through (both corporately and personally) has prepared you for the greatest season of fruitfulness and blossoming you've ever experienced. Watch as the early signs of His purpose and plans for your life begin to unfold in the coming days. Can you not discern this new day of destiny breaking forth around you?

I am doing something brand new, something unheard of. **Even now** *it sprouts and grows and matures. Don't you perceive it?...*
- Isaiah 43:19a TPT

To perceive or discern something means to realize, to become aware of, or to become conscious of that thing. The King is baiting us into a *realization*, an *awareness*, and a *knowing* in this season. Things have shifted and changed in your life, and He wants you to perceive and discern the change. Though you may not see any tangible, outward evidence in this very moment, the Lord says – it's a new day of destiny for you and your season has changed. Go throughout today with great expectation, and posture your heart to perceive and experience the bursting forth of The King's purposes and plans for your life. Get excited, it's happening even now!

Prayer: *My King, I am so grateful for this Word of prophecy directly from Your Word. I say "yes and amen," and I come in full agreement with what You have declared over me in this season. I will not walk by sight but by faith, which is my evidence. Thank You for this new season! Thank You for this new day of destiny! Posture and ready my heart for all You have in store. It has been a long, hard, barren winter, but I attune my spiritual ears to now hear the cooing of the doves, signifying that my harvest is indeed ready. I decree and declare that I will emerge from this season with armloads of blessing and an overflowing harvest, for all the seed I've sown in tears. Thank You that nothing has been wasted!*

Conversation With The King

Day Twelve
"The Little Foxes"

The King: *You must catch the troubling foxes, those sly little foxes that hinder our relationship. For they raid our budding vineyard of love to ruin what I've planted within you. Will you catch them and remove them for Me? We will do it together.*
- Song of Solomon 2:15 TPT

In today's devotional reading, The King wants to address the "little foxes" that hinder our relationship with Him. He encourages The Shulamite to catch them and remove them; then He tells her, "We will do it together." You see, this process of cleansing, healing, and deliverance is not one that you have to go through alone. It's a loving partnership. Your King is willing and ready to join in it with you.

From a Biblical perspective, foxes tend to represent sins or sinful habits that attempt to destroy fruit and block fruitfulness. They are "little sins" that alert you to a deeper spiritual matter or issue – something that could easily be overlooked or mistaken for something else, if you are unable to quickly discern and address it. The King perhaps used the term "foxes" to refer to these, often overlooked, sins because of the spirit of deception that's involved. That reminds me of an experience I once had with a fox. I heard a woman screaming in the woods beside my house one night. It was a loud, piercing scream that greatly concerned me. I was on the verge of calling the police when I remembered that someone once told me that a *fox* sounds like a woman screaming. I immediately did a quick search on Google and found a video of a screaming fox that sounded exactly like the sound I heard coming from the woods! The experience was quite sobering as I could have been deceived by the sound, had I not been previously made aware of this characteristic of foxes.

In order to catch the foxes attempting to raid the vineyard and ruin what The King has planted in us, we have to first consider the characteristics of these foxes so that we know how to identify them. He first described them as "*little.*" That signifies something that's seemingly insignificant, or maybe even something that's in its beginning stages. Something that's easy to miss, overlook, or mistake for something else. This is important because we tend to miss or overlook little negative habits or practices that are in their embryonic stage in our lives. They are small, but harmful nonetheless (James 3:3-5). The wisdom in The King's plea is that we catch them while they are still small, before they become full-grown, mature, and out of control.

He goes on to tell The Shulamite that the little foxes "*ruin the vine.*" These little sins affect and hinder our relationship with The King. Not necessarily the big things, but those things we think are insignificant or "not a big deal." Foxes chew on and break the branches and leaves off plants; they dig holes in the vineyard and they spoil the roots. In other words, foxes can severely affect the harvest. They threaten our relationship with The King and threaten to ruin what we have built in the place of prayer. I believe, in addition to them representing sins, *foxes* also represent the false doctrines, wrong mindsets, and ungodly beliefs that unconsciously govern our lives. Are you beginning to understand why The King admonished The Shulamite – as He is admonishing us today – to catch them?

Beloved Shulamite, your King wants to help you to identify, catch, and remove the little foxes in order to secure the vine. There are little *foxes* – little issues, a little false teaching here, a little false teaching there, a little leaven here, a little leaven there, little offenses – that are threatening to hinder your relationship with The King, raid your budding vineyard of love, and ruin what He has planted in you. Will you let Him help you catch and remove them today? He says to you, assuredly – *"We will do it together!"*

Prayer: *O King of the vineyard of my heart, thank You today for speaking so tenderly to me. Please bring to the surface any hidden sin in my life. Shine the light of Your love into my heart today and expose those things I have been excusing or overlooking. I partner with You in identifying, catching, and removing them, in Jesus Name. Please forgive me for the times I have played catch-and-release with these little foxes, not realizing that they are destroying the very harvest I prayed for. I pray for a replenishing and new growth to every branch, leaf, root, and fruit that has been damaged by little foxes in my heart. Please help me secure the borders of our vineyard and repair every breach. Thank You for fiercely protecting everything You've planted in me.*

Conversation With The King

Day Thirteen
"Another Time"

The Shulamite: *I know my Lover is mine and I have everything in You, for we delight ourselves in each other. But until the day springs to life and the shifting shadows of fear disappear, turn around, my Lover, and ascend to the holy mountains of separation without me. Until the new day fully dawns, run on ahead like the graceful gazelle and skip like the young stag over the mountains of separation. Go on ahead to the mountain of spices – I'll come away another time.*
- Song of Solomon 2:16-17 TPT

These verses in Song of Solomon are two of the most sobering verses in the entire book. We read yesterday that The King lovingly invited The Shulamite to catch and remove the little foxes that threatened to destroy their relationship. He even offered for them to do it together. Today we read that The Shulamite recognizes that, with The King, she can indeed do anything! She acknowledges in the sixteenth verse (above), that she *knows* that she has *everything* in Him – meaning, she is not lacking or missing anything in Him. Yet, at the thought of catching the little foxes and coming away with Him, she becomes fearful and rejects His invitation.

"I'll come away another time."

Isn't that just like us as God's Shulamite Bride? We're with Him until it costs us something; until we have to leave everything behind.

Verse seventeen begins with the word, *"Until..."* The Shulamite was unwilling to come away with the King *until* the old season had completely ended and the new season had fully begun. How many times have you prayed a *"God-if-You-do-this-then-I'll-do-that"* kind of prayer? The Shulamite's conditions had to be met first, before she would fully commit to going away with The King. He loved her unconditionally, but her willingness to commit to going away with Him – to leaving everything behind for Him – was conditional. We reject God so often out of fear of the unknown, or fear of losing the known.

Just a couple of verses prior (verses 8-9), The Shulamite took pleasure in the fact that her King climbed over mountains and hills to get to her. Now, because of her fear, uncertainty, and feelings of inadequacy, she's telling Him to go back to the "mountain of separation" – the very place He just traveled from to be with her.

But until the day springs to life and the shifting shadows of fear disappear, turn around, my Lover, and ascend to the holy mountains of separation without me.

Does your heart currently hold the same posture as The Shulamite's? Are you afraid of abandoning everything to make that next level of commitment to The King? He did more than climb over mountains and hills to get to us – He *died* for our sins. He died for the very fear that prevents us from committing fully to Him. Think about that today.

The King invited The Shulamite (as He invites you today) to come away with Him. He affirmed her and told her how much He loved her, and how beautiful she was to Him, despite her flaws. Yet, she rejected Him. Pushed Him away. Told Him that she could not be with Him until everything was perfect and all the conditions were met. This Shulamite is you and me, today. Our King welcomes us with open arms and showers us with unconditional love – yet, conditions of worth that we have experienced in relationships with significant others in our lives, tell us that we're not good enough for this kind of love. Conditions of worth tell us that we have to meet certain prerequisites and conditions for love, in order to be loved. And in true human nature, we project how people treat us onto our loving King who is not even human (Numbers 23:19), and who does not possess the capacity for evil (1 John 1:5).

Beloved Shulamite, The King's invitation still stands today. Let's push past fear and take Him up on His offer. It's one we will never regret!

Prayer: *Beloved King, I confess my fears to You today. I confess all the "things" that make me hesitate to follow You and give You my full commitment. Please forgive me and help me in these areas. I want to live a sold-out life for You. I want to come away with You. Please search my heart today and lovingly confront those secret, hidden issues. I'm understanding all the more why You admonish me to catch and remove the little foxes. I'm ready, Dôḏî. Today is the day. Let's go!*

Conversation With The King

Day Fourteen
"I Must Rise"

The Shulamite: *Night after night I'm tossing and turning on my bed of travail. Why did I let Him go from me? How my heart now aches for Him, but He is nowhere to be found! So, I must rise in search of Him, looking throughout the city, seeking until I find Him. Even if I have to roam through every street, nothing will keep me from my search. Where is He – my soul's True Love? He is nowhere to be found.*
- Song of Solomon 3:1-2 TPT

After deciding to send The King away because of her own fears and insecurities, The Shulamite now regrets her decision. Have you ever unintentionally rejected God and immediately regretted it? There are times in our walk with God where we reject Him and He seems distant or even missing. These are the hardest times to navigate as we often question His love for us and retrace our steps to determine where we went wrong, or where we may have missed Him. When it seems like God is nowhere to be found, how we respond or react matters far more than the times we sense His presence near us. This is because there is always the temptation to give up and let go in moments when God seems missing or distant. How do you tend to respond when you can't find (sense) God?

The Shulamite describes her utter distress when she realizes that she cannot find her King. After nights of tossing, turning, and travailing – after dealing with heartache and bitter regret – she decides that she *has* to go looking for Him. Beloved Shulamite, that is the posture The King wants us to have when we can't sense Him near us. He wants us to come after Him, not pull away.

> *Then [with a deep longing] you will seek Me and require Me [as a vital necessity] and [you will] find Me when you search for Me with all your heart.*
> - Jeremiah 29:13 AMP

The Shulamite was determined that nothing would hinder her search for her soul's True Love. If you are currently in a place where you feel like God has gone silent and you're tempted to give up and let go, I want to encourage you to *rise and keep searching.* Remember, this is the same King who climbed over hills and mountains for you; certainly, He is worthy of mutual pursuit. It doesn't matter what you did to reject or displease Him. It doesn't matter how far away you feel like you are, or He is. Don't allow condemnation, guilt, or shame to have the last word. Let nothing keep you from your search!

When The Shulamite said she looked throughout "the city," this represents the local church. It makes sense that the Church would be the first place she would look for The King. You may be one today who has searched for God even in the Church, but have not been able to find Him. Like Mary at the tomb, you may be saying, *"They have taken my Lord away and I don't know where He is."* (John 20:13). You may feel frustrated, discouraged, and hopeless about ever feeling the connection you used to feel to Him, or ever feeling the connection others have described. Your search for God, even in the Church, may have proven futile. You may feel like The Shulamite today that *He is nowhere to be found.*

I want to encourage you to keep searching, knowing that God is never lost! Even when you don't sense His presence, He is there (Hebrews 13:5b). At times when He seems hidden, this provides the opportunity to seek Him with a deeper longing. He longs to fill you with more and more of Himself; but only empty vessels have the capacity to be filled. Your diligent searching for Him creates an emptiness and a desperate hunger and longing for Him that He will soon satisfy! Beloved Shulamite, no matter how many times you've rejected The King, He is waiting for you to rise in search of Him. Today, let nothing keep you from your search!

Prayer: *My soul's True Love, I press into You today. How my heart and soul long and ache for You! Please forgive me for the ways and times I have rejected Your invitation to come away with You. Please allow Yourself to be found by me as I seek You diligently and with all my heart. I will let nothing keep me from my search. Every day of my life, I must rise in search of You. May I never reject Your invitation again. Expand my capacity for more and more of You as I seek You daily. Fill me to the point of overflow. I yield myself fully and completely to You today. I say, here I am, Lord!*

Conversation With The King

Day Fifteen
"I Found The One"

The Shulamite: *Then I encountered the overseers as they encircled the city. So I asked them, "Have you found Him – my heart's True Love?" Just as I moved past them, I encountered Him. I found the One I adore! I caught Him and fastened myself to Him, refusing to be feeble in my heart again. Now I'll bring Him back to the temple within where I was given new birth – into my innermost parts, the place of my conceiving.*
- Song of Solomon 3:3-4 TPT

What absolute joy we experience when we are reconciled with our King after a period of perceived separation! The Shulamite searched high and low, and could not contain herself when she found her heart's True Love. In order to find Him, she had to push past a certain hindrance that, if she was not careful, would have prevented her reconnection with The King. I believe this is a warning for us today, to be mindful of this particular hindrance that threatens real relationship with God. I'm talking about the spirit of religion.

I wrote a book in 2014 titled, "Moving From Religion To Relationship," and in it I detailed my personal testimony of how God saved me from a life of religion and legalism, and ushered me into true relationship with Him. The Shulamite could not locate her King "throughout the city," meaning in the local church, so she kept on searching. In today's reading we see where she finds her King "just as she moved past" the overseers who were encircling the city (Song of Solomon 3:4 TPT). *The overseers* can represent legalism or a religious spirit that we have to be determined to move past in order to find The

King. If your walk with God is based primarily on rules or a list of do's and don'ts, then you have yet to "move past the overseers." Our walk with The King is not meant to be based on rules and legalism, but on the freedom that Jesus Christ died for us to have (Isaiah 61:1) and the full, abundant life He promised (John 10:10b).

So, how do we walk and live in true relationship with The King? We grab hold of Him and fasten ourselves to Him, as The Shulamite did. We do this by ensuring that nothing comes between us and our King, and we strengthen our hearts in prayer and intimate fellowship with Him. To walk even more closely, The Shulamite references yet another way to stay in relationship with The King:

Now I'll bring Him back to the temple within.... into my innermost parts...

We invite Him into the temple of our hearts and into the very secret places where our desires and thoughts are conceived. That is the level of intimacy afforded us through deep relationship with The King. Beloved Shulamite, religion could never offer that!

The reason The Shulamite was able to find The King was because He allowed Himself to be found by her. And today, He is doing the same for you. As you continue to pursue Him and to search for Him, moving past the things that hinder – He will be found by you. He is in no way withholding Himself from you.

The lesson today is to hold on to The King with all your mind, soul, and strength; and fasten your heart to Him. Live in that oneness of continual relationship with Him so that nothing and no one can come between. Bring Him back today to the temple of your heart and allow Him access to the places where your desires are born. He wants that level of intimate relationship with you. Have you found The One today? Are you ready to hug Him and sink down into His arms? He's waiting to be found by you.

Prayer: *My Beloved King, truly You are The One! Thank You for never withholding Yourself from me, but allowing Yourself to be found by me. I fasten my heart to You today. I invite You into my temple within; into the innermost parts, to the place of my conceiving. I give You full access to every vault of my heart. Help me to not let anything separate us – not even religion. Give me the strength to move past anything that threatens to hinder our relationship. May I never be feeble in my heart again. I choose You above everything today, tomorrow, and for the rest of my life.*

Conversation With The King

Day Sixteen
"Who Is This One?"

Who is this One ascending from the wilderness in the pillar of the glory cloud? He is fragrant with the anointing oils of myrrh and frankincense – more fragrant than all the spices of the merchant.
- Song of Solomon 3:6 TPT

Beloved Shulamite, I want to start off today's devotional reading by encouraging you with the obvious: The King could only have ascended *from* the wilderness because He was *in* the wilderness in the first place! He wants you to know today that He is with you even in the barren, dry, and isolating seasons of your life. Wherever you find yourself today, regardless of how painful or embarrassing it may be, He is there right now.

Where could I go from Your Spirit? Where could I run and hide from Your face? If I go up to Heaven, You're there. If I go down to the realm of the dead, You're there too! If I fly with wings into the shining dawn, You're there! If I fly into the radiant sunset, You're there waiting!
- Psalm 139:7-9 TPT

Not only is He with you wherever you are so you never have to face anything alone; He is also with you to lead you out in triumph. He ascended from the wilderness in *the pillar of the glory cloud*. I could not help but think about "the cloud by day and the pillar of fire by night" (Exodus 13:21) as I read this verse. When the Israelites were travelling through the wilderness, the Lord led them from place to place by a cloud by day and a pillar of fire by night. This represented His presence and His divine direction. Know today that as you walk through your wilderness season, His glory cloud is pointing the way that you should go. He is not going to let you miss it. You are never without help or direction, not even when in the wilderness!

Now let's talk about what The King smells like as He's with you in the wilderness seasons of your life. He is described as *fragrant* – the anointing oils of myrrh and frankincense are specifically mentioned as a part of His fragrance. Myrrh tends to represent suffering and frankincense represents Christ's life and ministry. The fact that these two fragrances are referenced is significant, because they show that our King is not only anointed in life and ministry, but also in the area of suffering. He not only understands suffering – He is anointed with it! This is why you can trust Him with your hurt and pain, because He is fully acquainted with grief (Isaiah 53:3). When He died for you on the Cross, He bore the pain of everything that would *ever* hurt you in your entire life. *Selah*.

There is no pain or hurt that you will ever experience that your King has not already experienced for you. He is not a High Priest who is unable to sympathize and understand our weaknesses, but He knows exactly how it feels to be human in every respect as we are (Hebrews 4:15 AMP). This is *The One* who has positioned Himself in your current situation.

I don't know where you may find yourself today. You may be in your own personal wilderness wondering if God has forsaken you, or if He even cares. I pray that your heart is encouraged to know that, not only is He with you right where you are in this very moment, but that He knows exactly how you feel. You are His Beloved! If you're there, He's there. If you're feeling it, He's feeling it. He is *more fragrant* than all the spices of the merchant. No one else wears the fragrances that He does, because no one has ever done what He has done

(John 3:16), or endured what He has endured (Hebrews 12:2). Of all the places that He is at any given time – as our Omnipresent God – He positions Himself in the wilderness *with* you and *for* you. May your heart find rest in that reassurance today, Beloved Shulamite!

Prayer: *My Good Shepherd, I thank You today for being in the wilderness with me to comfort and rescue me. No matter where I find myself, I never walk alone because You are always with me. Thank You for Your glory cloud that points the way that I should go. I'm so grateful to have You as my Guide. Thank You for understanding exactly how I feel in this moment. Sometimes the seasons become so painful that I don't know how I'm going to make it. But, today I smell the frankincense and myrrh as I walk with You, and that reminds me that You've already conquered everything for me. Indeed, You are more fragrant than all the spices of the merchant! I rest in the fragrance of Your love today.*

Conversation With The King

Day Seventeen
"The Mercy Seat"

Look! It is The King's marriage carriage – the love seat surrounded by sixty champions, the mightiest of Israel's host, are like the pillars of protection. The King made this mercy seat for Himself out of the finest wood that will not decay.
- Song of Solomon 3:7, 9 TPT

Beloved Shulamite, when riding with The King in His marriage carriage – a reflection of the intimate relationship you share with Him – you are protected by the host of Angel Armies. You never have to fear harm or danger when you are travelling with your King. One of His names is Tsaba: The Lord of Hosts, or The God of Angel Armies. He is the Commander-in-Chief of Heaven and earth, and you can rest assured that you are forever covered and protected by Him. Life sometimes takes us on difficult paths that may cause us fear or angst, but if we keep this Truth safely tucked away in our hearts – that we are surrounded by His *pillars of protection* – then we'd realize we truly have no reason to fear.

God, You're such a safe and powerful place to find refuge! You're a proven Help in time of trouble – more than enough and always available whenever I need You. So [I] will not fear even if every structure of support were to crumble away. [I] will not fear even when the earth quakes and shakes, moving mountains and casting them into the sea.
- Psalm 46:1-2 TPT [brackets mine]

In this marriage carriage that is surrounded by His pillars of protection, there is the mercy seat upon which The

Shulamite sits with her Beloved King. It's first called the *love* seat, then it's referred to as the *mercy* seat. They are one and the same. Beloved Shulamite, God's love is His mercy and His mercy is His love. When you are in relationship with Him, you have access to both and as you traverse the different terrains of life, your seat is secure in His love and mercy.

The mercy seat in The King's marriage carriage is described as being made of the finest wood that cannot decay. That may not mean much to you if you are a person who rarely messes up or makes mistakes. But, if you (like me) have fallen more times than you can count, the thought that The King's seat of mercy is made from wood that can never decay, is like a cool drink on a hot summer day! Because His mercy cannot break down, break up, wither, or deteriorate – *ever* – that means it will *never* run out and is always accessible to us. Regardless of how many times you stand in need of His mercy, it is available to you because it never decays. Are you in need of mercy today? Go boldly to your King, climb up in His marriage carriage, and take your rest in the *mercy seat* reserved for you!

...Mercy triumphs [victoriously] over judgment.
- James 2:13b AMP

Beloved Shulamite, your King knew you would need mercy often in this life, so He built the mercy seat strong. It can bear the weight of the darkest confession and it provides you with the authority needed to stand against the wiles and strategies of the adversary. The King's mercy towards you gives you authority over anything that opposes your freedom in Him. Climb up today and rest. Take your rightful seat as a joint-heir with Christ.

I call you out of shame, guilt, grief, condemnation, regret, and sadness today, in the Name of Jesus! I command the chains that have been holding you captive to loose you now! I decree and declare that you are free in Jesus Name! Assume your position of authority in The King's mercy seat. Walk in that freedom today. Walk in His love. Walk in His mercy, Beloved Shulamite!

Prayer: *Merciful King, I thank You today that You built the mercy seat strong for me. Thank You that Your mercy never decays and Your love never runs out. I have lived my life at times as if I have used up all Your mercy. But, thank You for this timely reminder today that there is always more love and mercy reserved for me. May I forever cherish my seat with You. Help me to never take advantage of my position or my place in You. I receive Your love and mercy. Today, I walk in my authority, boldly, by faith.*

Conversation With The King

Day Eighteen
"You Are Beauty Itself"

The Bridegroom-King: *Listen, My dearest darling, you are so beautiful – you are beauty itself to Me! Your eyes are like gentle doves behind your veil. What devotion I see each time I gaze upon you. You are like a sacrifice ready to be offered. When I look at you, I see how you have taken My fruit and tasted My word. Your life has become clean and pure, like a lamb washed and newly shorn. You now show grace and balance with truth on display.*
- Song of Solomon 4:1-2 TPT

Today, The King wants to just shower His love and affection on you. He wants to overwhelm you with words of affirmation, which is one of His many love languages. Would you read the verses again? And, this time, insert your name in the first verse where He says, "*My dearest darling* <insert name>..." Indeed, Beloved Shulamite, you are beauty itself to Him. He is not just saying this because these are nice words to say – our King cannot lie! (Numbers 23:19, Hebrews 6:18).

If you have struggled in the past with feeling like God is an angry God, or One who is out to get you, then you may have a difficult time internalizing what He is expressing to you today. Yes, you may have made a million mistakes in life (so far), but The King sees your devotion to Him each time He looks at you. All you see are the mistakes you've made and all the ways you've messed up. But, He sees the gentleness of your eyes and the love you have for Him deep in your heart.

Whenever our hearts make us feel guilty and remind us of our failures, we know that God is much greater and more merciful

> *than our conscience, and He knows everything there is to know about us.*
> - 1 John 3:20 TPT

Even as you have made your way to Day Eighteen of these 31 Days of Intimacy with The King, He sees how you have taken His fruit and tasted His Word (Song of Solomon 4:2 TPT). As you have read each devotional reading and engaged in your own conversation with The King, He has taken delight in your heart of pursuit for Him. As you have meditated on His Word and applied the conversations He had with The Shulamite to your own life, your life has become clean and pure. It is the Truth of His Word that sanctifies (John 17:17). You have been *sanctified* these past eighteen days and He will continue to sanctify you with His Truth in the remaining twelve days of this 31-day journey.

The King calls you beautiful today. He finds no fault in you, despite the faults you may find in yourself. His thoughts about you are so much higher than the thoughts you think about yourself. Your highest thought of you is His lowest thought of you! Today, He invites you into *His* thoughts of you. Imagine what it would be like if you went through each day *only* thinking God's thoughts toward you!

In fact, let's commit to giving that a try today – to meditating on these first two verses in this fourth chapter of Song of Solomon, and allowing *only* what The King has said to permeate our minds. You may not be able to fully agree with His expressions because of where you find yourself, or how you see yourself. But, if *He* magnifies His Word above His very name, then you should too. Today, let's magnify His beautiful words about us together!

I will worship toward Your holy Temple, and praise Your Name for Your lovingkindness and Your Truth. For You have magnified Your Word above all Your Name.
- Psalm 138:2 NKJV

Prayer: *My Bridegroom-King, I am overwhelmed by Your expression of love for me. I must admit that it's a bit hard to receive when I consider all I've done. I've messed up so many times. But, if You magnify Your Word above everything else, then so will I! Help me not to live according to how I feel, but according to what You said (Matthew 4:4). Hold the mirror of Your Word to my face today and help me to gaze deeply into Your Truth about me. As I closely examine Your Truth, may it set me free. Give me the grace I need to think only Your thoughts of me today; and may this become a lifestyle for me. Help me to walk in full agreement with You – even in my thoughts.*

Conversation With The King

Day Nineteen
"Inner Strength"

The Bridegroom-King: *When I look at you, I see your inner strength, so stately and strong. You are as secure as David's fortress. Your virtues and grace cause a thousand famous soldiers to surrender to your beauty.*
- Song of Solomon 4:4 TPT

Inner strength refers to a sense of resoluteness, fortitude, and resistance to discouragement or doubt. It is inner strength, more than physical strength, that enables us to navigate challenges in life and bounce back when we've been knocked down. You may not feel physically strong today, but that is no reflection of the strength you have on the inside. Today, The King wants to celebrate your *inner* strength.

So, no wonder we don't give up. For even though our outer person gradually wears out, our inner being is renewed every single day.
- 2 Corinthians 4:16 TPT

The King describes you as stately, strong, and secure like David's fortress. A fortress is like a stronghold that serves as a defensive structure and a refuge in the time of war. The King is saying to you today that you are strong and He has even created you to serve as a place of refuge for others. You may not feel like this at the moment, but The King *built* you with inner strength and He's speaking to what He knows is inside of you! The purpose of these 31 Days of Intimacy is to establish and settle our identity in The King's love for us and *His* opinion of us. We have to see ourselves the way He sees us, as *that's the Truth.* Anything outside of that is a lie.

Beloved Shulamite, you were built to handle all you've experienced (and will experience) in life. You were built to last! Although the outside circumstances seem to be wearing away at you – mentally, physically, spiritually, and emotionally – you have been built solid at your core. How else do you think you've been able to make it through all the hell you've been through so far? Have you ever considered that? It could only have been God's strength and grace! And, even as He calls you a fortress of defense against all that has come against you in this life, He also desires that you become that fortress of refuge for others who are now where you have been. Who can you encourage and uplift today as they walk through some of the same painful experiences you have overcome?

Even in this moment, The King is beautifying you. He is continuing to work on the areas of your heart and life where you continue to struggle. But, even though you are still in-progress, He speaks of you as though you were complete (Isaiah 42:9) – telling you that *the most famous soldiers will surrender to your beauty.* What God is doing, even in this very moment, is going to cause the strongest opponent or opposition to melt at the beautiful work He is performing in you.

He has made everything beautiful and appropriate in its time.
- Ecclesiastes 3:11a AMP

Commit to coming in agreement with The King's thoughts about you. He has given you inner strength, virtue, grace, and absolute beauty. Surrender to all He is currently doing in your life and walk in the confidence that everything He has spoken concerning you is as good as done! (Isaiah 46:11b).

Prayer: *King of my heart, I thank You today for building me strong. I don't always feel strong – in fact, most days I struggle to feel any ounce of strength. But, I thank You that my feelings aren't truth, but Your Word is Truth. Give me the grace to keep moving forward even when it feels like my strength is failing. Cause my inner man to be renewed today and may Your strength be made perfect in my weakness. I look to You for everything that I need today. You are my Strong Tower and I run fully into You (Proverbs 18:10).*

Conversation With The King

Day Twenty
"I Will Go"

The Shulamite: *I've made up my mind. Until the darkness disappears and the dawn has fully come; in spite of shadows and fears, I will go to the mountaintop with You – the mountain of suffering love and the hill of burning incense. Yes, I will be Your bride.*
- Song of Solomon 4:6 TPT

The Shulamite is thoroughly convinced of The King's love for her and is beginning to see who she is to Him. So, now she expresses a willingness to go with Him wherever this love may take her – whether to the *mountain of suffering* or the *hill of burning incense*. The Shulamite has finally accepted The King's marriage proposal and has agreed to be His wife.

This was the same Shulamite in Day Thirteen who refused The King's invitation to come away with Him. She wanted to wait until all conditions were perfect before committing to all that being His bride involved. But, as we have read over the past seven days, The King has consistently poured out His love to her, showering her with words of affirmation and encouragement. And, in response to His love, The Shulamite now feels ready and has made up her mind – *I will go*.

"Coming away" with The King is not always an easy journey. Sometimes it involves the mountain of suffering love, which is our own personal Gethsemane or Calvary, where we have to suffer with Him (2 Timothy 2:12) and take up our own crosses (Luke 9:23). The King knows this is challenging, so He encourages us to count the cost.

So, don't follow Me without considering what it will cost you. For who would construct a house before first sitting down to estimate the cost to complete it?
- Luke 14:28 TPT

The beauty about taking this journey with Him, however, is the fact that we never have to face any mountain of suffering alone. He promises to be with us every step of the way (Hebrews 13:5b) and tells us that it is in our times of weakness that His strength is perfected (2 Corinthians 12:9).

The journey doesn't just lead us to the mountain of suffering love, it also leads us to the hill of burning incense. This speaks of worship and consecration. As we walk with The King, we draw closer and closer to Him in worship and through a consecrated life. This *hill* is where we die to ourselves and sacrifice anything that threatens to separate us from Him. The aroma that results from the burning is what sets us apart as His bride. People encounter us and they know that there is something different about us because we carry the smell of *burning incense*. Beloved Shulamite, The King's desire is for your life to be a sweet-smelling fragrance in His nostrils as you walk in deeper intimacy with Him.

Where do you find yourself today? Have you recently committed to being The King's bride? Are you currently counting the cost? Have you been walking with Him for some time and have found yourself on the mountain of suffering love today? Are you currently on the hill of incense? Wherever you find yourself in your journey with The King, know that He is right there with you. You are never alone. Like The Shulamite, be resolved in your mind today that no matter what happens – you will go.

Prayer: *My Bridegroom-King, it's taken me a while to get to this place in You. Thank You for being so patient with me. My desire today is to go all the way with You. Wherever the journey takes me, I am all in and I am all Yours. Please strengthen my heart on this journey with You. Whether I'm on the mountain of suffering love or the hill of incense, may I always feel You with me. May I be assured of Your grace and love. Deal with any area of fear in me today. Any area where I still struggle in my commitment. I confess these areas to You and ask for Your help and mercy. Here I am, today. I've made up my mind. I will go. I will be Your bride.*

Conversation With The King

Day Twenty-One
"Now You Are Ready"

The Bridegroom-King: *Every part of you is so beautiful, My darling. Perfect is your beauty, without flaw within. Now you are ready, My bride, to come with Me as we climb the highest peaks together. Come with Me through the archway of trust... For you reach into My heart. With one flash of your eyes, I am undone by your love, My beloved, My equal, My bride. You leave Me breathless – I am overcome by merely a glance from your worshiping eyes, for you have stolen My heart. I am held hostage by your love...*

- Song of Solomon 4:7-9 TPT

Today's verses are the perfect love letter. They are worth reading over and over and over again – and I hope you do just that! Yesterday, we read of how The Shulamite abandoned her insecurities and fears, and finally decided to commit fully to "coming away" with The King. In today's reading, we see His overwhelming response.

The King is so thrilled by The Shulamite's commitment to Him that it moves Him to dote on her all the more. He invites her to climb *the highest peaks* with Him – a symbol of elevation, expansion, and honor – an invitation afforded to all of us as we commit fully to His leading. Beloved Shulamite, The King wants you to know today that your eyes have not yet seen all that He has in store for you! There is so much more that He wants to reveal to you on this intimate journey. There are heights that you have not yet discovered or explored in Him, that are yet reserved for you as He beckons you to, "Come."

Come through the archway of trust. That word "archway" is the Hebrew word, "Amana," which means a place of settled security. The archway of trust is a place we all must pass through as we journey with The King. It involves complete surrender and trust in His perfect plan and way, even when we don't know or understand all that He's doing. It is a place of settled security, where we no longer wonder or wander – it's a place of rest. The King invites you today to come with Him through the crest of Amana; to reach into His very heart so that you can find true rest. We all need rest in this time. Will you enter in today? There is divine rest reserved just for you.

The King goes on to talk about The Shulamite's eyes and how just a look from her ravishes His heart, and leaves Him undone. Beloved Shulamite, it may be hard for you to believe today, but your King's heart is completely ravished whenever you look to Him in worship. He becomes vulnerable to you in these intimate moments when He is the focus of your attention. You unravel Him. Think about that for a minute. The King of Kings allows Himself to become vulnerable to us, His Shulamite Bride, when we draw close to Him in intimate worship. Even in our weakness and our shame, when we lock eyes with Him, *He* becomes undone. What a love! Recognize today that your King is absolutely obsessed with you. He sees you as flawlessly beautiful. *You have stolen His heart and He is held hostage by your love.*

There is nothing that someone who loves you that much won't do for you! Don't you see? He made the ultimate sacrifice in dying on the cross in our place (John 3:16) and spends every day of our lives proving His love to us. It breaks His heart when we don't see ourselves the way He sees us. When we settle for cheap, fake versions of "love" and abandon the place of intimate worship with our True Love.

The King is calling for a great return of His Bride today – to return to that place of intimate worship. To enter into His archway of trust and be willing to rest in His perfect love that drives out every trace of fear (1 John 4:18). He is speaking words of affirmation over you today. He has seen your heart's posture towards Him these twenty-one days and He says to you in this very moment: *Now you are ready!* Receive His decree, embrace it, and walk in it today!

Prayer: *King of my heart, I gaze into Your eyes today with eyes of adoration and worship. I pour myself out as a drink offering before You. Let my worship ravish Your heart today as I draw closer and closer to You. I want my heartbeat to be synchronized with Yours. I don't want to miss a beat. I enter in with You through the archway of trust today. I surrender all my cares and fears, and I choose instead to rest in You. Yes, I am ready, my King. Ready to go all the way with You.*

Conversation With The King

Day Twenty-Two
"Spare Nothing"

The Shulamite: *Awake, O north wind! Awake, O south wind! Breathe on my garden with Your Spirit-Wind. Stir up the sweet spice of Your life within me. Spare nothing as You make me Your fruitful garden. Hold nothing back until I release Your fragrance. Come walk with me as You walked with Adam in Your paradise garden. Come taste the fruits of Your life in me.*
- Song of Solomon 4:16 TPT

The Shulamite's response to The King's invitation to enter into the archway of trust is one of complete and utter surrender. Her response is like a prayer of life-dedication to her King. This same Shulamite who started off so timid, so hesitant, and so insecure, has been transformed as she has discovered and internalized The King's love for her. Beloved Shulamite, that is exactly what is happening to you as you press into these 31 days of intimacy – discovering your *true* identity that is only found in The King's love. Let's examine The Shulamite's prayer of surrender today.

Stir up the sweet spice of Your life within me. In Days Five and Sixteen, we talked about some of The King's spices – myrrh and frankincense; and how He uses all the experiences of our lives to create the perfect aroma that is released as incense when we worship. As The Shulamite asks The King to stir up the sweet spice of His life within her, she is asking for an even deeper level of intimacy with Him. Recognize today that The King has experienced and endured much for you – His life is filled with various *spices* reflecting all He's done and all He is. As He stirs up the sweet spice of His life within us, He is allowing us to experience all of who He is. There is always so much more to know and experience about The King at any given point in time. You can have as much of Him as you want. Will you pray like The Shulamite that He stirs up the sweet spice of His life within you today?

Spare nothing as You make me Your fruitful garden. As a pursuer of The King's heart, there comes a point in your life where you begin to desire more. Where the ordinary no longer satisfies. Where you long to be baited into deeper depths of His love, as your deep calls out to His deep (Psalm 42:7). It is at this point that you realize that nothing matters but your relationship with Him. Where no sacrifice is too great and no demand/request too high. This is where The Shulamite finds herself as she tells The King to *spare nothing* as He works on her to make her into His fruitful garden – into everything He has called her to be. Is that your heart's desire today? May The King spare nothing as He conforms us into His image and causes our lives to reflect Him, in Jesus Name!

Hold nothing back until I release Your fragrance. As The King's Shulamite-bride, there is a fragrance that we carry to the world. We look, walk, talk, act, think, and even *smell* differently. We represent our King in everything that we do and we serve as His reflection in the earth. This heart-yearning of The Shulamite is one of the most powerful "prayers" in the Bible. She asks The King to hold nothing back until her life releases His fragrance. That is the heart of true surrender. Where it doesn't matter how much crushing or pressing we have to go through in order to release the oil of His glory and presence. We're willing to pay the price because we love Him so desperately.

Come walk with me… come taste the fruits of Your life in me. That is our ultimate desire as The King's Bride. For Him to walk with us and taste the fruits of His life in us. That our lives demonstrate the fruit of Holy Spirit and reflect our communion with Him. That others may taste and see that the Lord – our King – is good! (Psalm 34:8).

The Shulamite has given us the perfect prayer to pray through and meditate on today. May Holy Spirit breathe on your garden even now, Beloved Shulamite. May The King stir up the sweet spice of His life within you. May He spare nothing as He makes you His fruitful garden. May He hold nothing back until you release His fragrance!

Prayer: *My Beloved King, I want to be everything that You have called me to be. I must admit that The Shulamite's prayer is overwhelming and I wonder if I'll ever get to that level in You. But, here I am today. If I've learned anything on this journey, it's that my feelings rarely ever reflect Your Truth about me. So, I choose to stand in Your Truth today and to pray this same prayer, in boldness, as Your Shulamite-bride. I trust You to come walk with me as You did with Adam, Moses, and Enoch, as You make me Your fruitful garden. Come taste the fruits of Your life in me today.*

Conversation With The King

Day Twenty-Three
"Deeper Still"

The Bridegroom-King: *Arise, My love. Open your heart, My darling, deeper still to Me. Will you receive Me this dark night? There is no one else but you, My friend, My equal. I need you this night to arise and come be with Me. You are My pure, loyal dove, a perfect partner for Me. My flawless one, will you arise? For My heaviness and tears are more than I can bear. I have spent Myself for you throughout the dark night.*
- Song of Solomon 5:2b TPT

There are times in life where we all have to walk through "dark nights of the soul" experiences. Whether it's the darkness of an unknown season, the pain of a challenging season, or a season of grief and loss. Life circumstances sometimes knock the wind out of us. In today's reading, The King is beckoning The Shulamite to open her heart *deeper still* to Him and to receive Him even in the "dark night." That is such a significant request because, more often than not, dark nights tend to pull us away from The King, rather than push us closer to Him. When going through seasons where we can't sense or feel Him – or we don't understand the pain He allows – we can be tempted to fall for the lie that He has abandoned us or is unmoved by what we're going through. It's at these times that we need to press in deeper, not pull away. If you currently find yourself in a dark night season, The King is baiting you into an even deeper and more intimate relationship with Him. He wants deeper access to your heart. Will you receive Him this dark night?

Regardless of the difficulty of the season or test, The King's love for you remains the same. He calls you His darling, His friend, His equal, His loyal dove, His perfect partner, and His flawless one. Take a moment to let those descriptions really sink deep into your heart. *This* is how your King sees you, even in the dark night season you may be going through! He's calling you to arise and to come be with Him. There are no to-do lists involved in this invitation. It's not an invitation to *do*, it's an invitation to *be*. If you were introduced to The Bridegroom-King from the standpoint of religion and not relationship, then you are used to a constant checklist of items to complete. Religion creates a performance and works-mentality that keeps us striving and slaving for something that The King has freely given us. Beloved Shulamite, The King just invites you today to *come and be*. You are enough for Him just as you are – no i's dotted, no t's crossed.

He goes on to tell The Shulamite that, while she has been dealing with her dark night season, He has "spent Himself" for her throughout this same dark night. Meaning, He has endured hardship, suffering, and pain (darkness) *for* her, to bring her *out* of the dark night she's experiencing. The King's heart is touched whenever your heart is tried, Beloved! There is nothing you will ever experience that He has not already experienced *for* you.

For My heaviness and tears are more than I can bear. I have spent Myself for you throughout the dark night.

Beloved Shulamite, your King has felt the heaviness and pain of every dark night you have experienced, and He has given His all for you.

And He said to them, "My heart is overwhelmed and crushed with grief. It feels as though I'm dying. Stay here and keep watch with Me."
- Matthew 26:38 TPT

The most fitting response to His love and sacrifice is to open your heart deeper still to Him today. Despite how difficult this season of your life has been, or the challenges you've had to face in the past – will you receive Him even in this? Will you allow dark nights of the soul to push you deeper into His arms, or pull you away? The choice is yours today as your Beloved King waits for your response.

Prayer: *My Beloved King, I open my heart deeper still to You today! I receive You in the darkness of this season; in the dark (unknown, painful, and ugly) areas of my life. I arise in the midst of the darkness and I come away with You! Thank You for "spending Yourself" for me throughout the dark night. Bethlehem, Gethsemane, and Calvary mean more to me than I could ever express! Thank You for all You endured in hardship, suffering, and pain for me. Thank You for never rejecting the bitter spice of myrrh. I love You with all my heart, my Friend, my Perfect Partner, my Flawless One!*

Conversation With The King

Day Twenty-Four
"My Soul Melted"

The Shulamite: *I have already laid aside my own garments for You. How could I take them up again since I've yielded my righteousness to Yours? You have cleansed my life and taken me so far. Isn't that enough? My Beloved reached into me to unlock my heart. The core of my very being trembled at His touch. How my soul melted when He spoke to me!*
- Song of Solomon 5:3-4 TPT

The Shulamite continues to press forward in her recommitment and rededication to The King. She reminds Him that she has laid aside her garments (her past or old self) for Him and that she would not take them up again (Luke 9:62). She reminds Him that she has yielded her righteousness to His as He has cleansed her life. What a beautiful picture of salvation! Because of Jesus' sacrifice on the cross of Calvary, you now have access to *His* righteousness. Your own righteousness – your highest attempt at being and doing right – is as a filthy rag before Him (Isaiah 64:6); so Jesus died for your sins in order that you could *become* the righteousness of God in Him!

For He made Him who knew no sin to be sin for us, that we might become the righteousness of God in Him. – 2 Corinthians 5:21 NKJV

As The Shulamite considers all of this, she becomes overwhelmed and asks the question, *"Isn't that enough?"* Isn't it enough that Jesus died for us and has made us righteous in Him? What more could we ever ask or expect from Him? Yet, our Beloved King continues to offer us more and more of Himself, as He baits us deeper still. The Shulamite gives us a visual of this *deeper still* kind of relationship.

My Beloved reached into me to unlock my heart. At times our hearts shut down or metaphorically retract in our chests because of the painful experiences we go through. There are many of us who actually fear anyone coming close to our hearts, for fear that we may end up getting hurt again. It is comforting to know though, in spite of our fears, that The One who designed and created our very hearts, holds the combination code that gives Him ultimate access. Beloved Shulamite, your King is never "locked out" of your heart. He knows how to unlock the most sealed areas of our hearts and lives, and He wants to do that for you today. You may be reading this and you may feel like your heart has been broken far too many times for you to ever open up to anyone again – including The King. Recognize that He knows exactly how you feel at this very moment and He knows how to meet you where you are.

You are so intimately aware of me, Lord. You read my heart like an open book...
- Psalm 139:3a TPT

The core of my soul trembled at His touch. This is the very definition of nakedness and vulnerability. That The Shulamite would allow The King complete access to her heart and soul, and that His touch would cause her soul – her mind, will, and emotions – to tremble. It's impossible to be touched by God and remain the same. Everything responds to His touch. He wants to touch your mind, your will, and your emotions today. He wants to bait you into that place of naked surrender and vulnerability. *That*, Beloved Shulamite, is the highest place of intimacy that we can experience with our King.

How my soul melted when He spoke to me! Not only does The King want your soul to tremble at His touch; He wants it to melt at His voice. Imagine being so intimately acquainted with The King – so sensitive to His touch and voice – that you experience a trembling and a melting in your every encounter with Him. Think about those worrisome thoughts that have been plaguing your mind lately. Those thoughts will tremble and melt away at one touch and one whisper from The King. That is the place in Him that He baits us into as He unlocks our hearts and calls us to come deeper still.

Take some time to meditate on this invitation into complete nakedness and vulnerability today. Be honest with The King about what could possibly hinder you from fully laying aside your garments and completely committing to a life of deeper intimacy with Him. He longs to melt your soul!

Prayer: *My Beloved King, You have my heart! I give You full access to all of me. The hidden parts, the broken parts, and the ugly parts. I desire to walk in naked and vulnerable intimacy with You. Come and melt my soul. Come and speak to the deep places within me. I am open to You.*

Conversation With The King

Day Twenty-Five
"I Endured All"

The Shulamite: *...Make me this promise, you brides-to-be; if you find my Beloved One, please tell Him I endured all travails for Him. I've been pierced through by love, and I will not be turned aside!*
Jerusalem Maidens, Brides-to-Be: *What love is this? How could you continue to care so deeply for Him? Isn't there another who could steal away your heart? We see now your beauty, more beautiful than all the others. What makes your Beloved better than any other? What is it about Him that makes you ask us to promise you this?*
- Song of Solomon 5:8-9 TPT

The Shulamite has just endured great affliction as she pressed deeper in her search for The King. She describes her encounter with "the overseers" (Song of Solomon 5:7) – who represent religion and a religious mindset – as they "beat and bruised her until she could take no more." Perhaps you can relate to The Shulamite's experience. You have encountered religion and the religious, and have been bruised and wounded as you have searched for a deeper relationship with The King. No matter what you've done, or how hard you've tried, you've been made to feel that your efforts aren't good enough to please The King. At times, despite being well-intentioned, religion can serve more as a *gatekeeper* than a *gateway*. With its rules, legalism, and performance-based mentality, it can feel like we are working for our salvation with no true freedom or rest. This can truly leave us feeling bruised and defeated. Praying your strength if this is where you find yourself today!

Despite her painful encounter with the overseers, The Shulamite remains persistent in her search for a deeper relationship with The King. She will not be turned aside! In desperation, she asks her *friends* – her fellow Brides-in-waiting – to intercede on her behalf. Perhaps she felt they had a closer relationship with The King than she did. Whatever her thoughts, she just wanted some support and encouragement in all she had endured for Him. But, instead of being met with that prayerful support and encouragement, The Jerusalem Maidens could not fathom her love for One who would cause her so much suffering.

For many are called (invited, summoned), but few are chosen.
– Matthew 22:14 AMP

Beloved Shulamite, not everyone is going to understand the intensity of your desire for deeper relationship with The King. Not everyone is going to understand the sacrifices you have made to truly live for Jesus. Many are invited into this *deeper still* relationship, but only few are chosen – only few actually respond. It is evident that The Jerusalem Maidens did not have the same level of commitment and dedication as The Shulamite. They were actually trying to dissuade her from her intense pursuit, because they could not understand her desire for a love that caused her to suffer.

There are many "Jerusalem Maidens" in the world today. These are those who walk with The King, but have limitations on how far they will go and what they will endure for His namesake.

*Therefore, I will save My flock, and they shall no longer be a prey; and I will judge between sheep and **sheep**.*
– Ezekiel 34: 22 NKJV

There are sheep and then there are *sheep*. Make sure you are in the right group of sheep. It is very critical in this season to be relentless in your desire for a deeper, more intimate relationship with The King. To not be deterred or dissuaded by anyone or anything. You will face opposition outside the walls of the church and you will face opposition right in the pews. Wherever the opposition comes from, are you prepared to defend your suffering love for The King?

The Jerusalem Maidens asked The Shulamite – *"Isn't there another who could steal away your heart?"* What would be your response to that question today, Beloved Shulamite? After all The King has done for you and all that you have endured for Him, what could separate you from His love today? Selah.

Prayer: *My Beloved King, I invite You to search me today. Please show me if there is anything in me or in my life that has the potential to steal away my heart. I confess any hidden idols that I may be unaware of. I dethrone them in Your presence and I declare that You are the Lord of all the kingdoms of my heart. Make me resolute in the face of criticism and persecution. Help me to stand on the Truth established in my heart. I decree and declare today that my heart belongs only to You. I have endured all travails for You. I have been pierced through by love, and I will not be turned aside. You are my choice forever!*

Conversation With The King

Day Twenty-Six
"None Like Him"

The Shulamite: *[12] He sees everything with pure understanding. How beautiful His insights – without distortion. His eyes rest upon the fullness of the river of revelation, flowing so clean and pure. [14] See how His hands hold unlimited power! But He never uses it in anger, for He is always holy, displaying His glory... [15] He's steadfast in all He does. His ways are the ways of righteousness, based on truth and holiness. None can rival Him. [16]... If you ask me why I love Him so, O brides-to-be, it's because there is none like Him to me...*

- Song of Solomon 5:12, 14-16
TPT

Yesterday, we ended with the question that The Jerusalem-Maidens asked The Shulamite regarding her suffering love for The King. Today, we will examine The Shulamite's response as she boasts about her King – to the extent that The Jerusalem-Maidens begin to express *their own* longing for Him (Song of Solomon 6:1). I decree and declare the same outcome for every time your relationship with The King is challenged. As you respond in love, may the hearts of all the "challengers" be filled with a longing for Him beyond anything they could have ever imagined, in Jesus Name!

In verse twelve of the fifth chapter of Song of Solomon, The Shulamite describes the perfection of The King's *sight* and His *insight*. Beloved Shulamite, God can never misunderstand you. He sees with perfect understanding and His insight has perfect and complete revelation. He never misinterprets anything you say or do, because He understands the motive and heart behind everything you say and do. There is nothing about you that The King does not know! While people may misunderstand your actions or misinterpret your words, your King never does (Psalm 139:1-2). Rest in the perfection of His insight and understanding of you today.

The Shulamite goes on to boast that The King's hands hold unlimited power, yet He never uses His power in anger. The King demonstrates such unending mercy and great restraint with you, Beloved Shulamite. He is always holy in His decisions and actions. Regardless of what you do, He will never deny Himself or His character in His response to you (2 Timothy 2:13). Think about that the next time you feel like "God is out to get you" or like He is punishing you for something you did in the past, for which you've already repented. Our King is not a human being (Numbers 23:19), so He is incapable of responding and acting as fickle as human beings do. And although He has all power to do whatever He wants, because of His unconditional love for you and the purity of His nature, He never uses that power against you in any way (Jeremiah 29:11).

In an ever-changing world, The Shulamite acknowledges that her King is steadfast (that is, consistent, determined, and stable) in all that He does. He is not double-minded, fickle, or shaky in His actions. That is why He can be trusted, Beloved Shulamite. He is a sure foundation and can withstand any change you may experience. In this season where many find themselves in transition, it may feel like the winds are blowing violently in your life. It may feel like everything is being shaken. If that is where you find yourself today, rest assured that your King cannot be shaken. He is steadfast and He holds you steady and firm in the palms of His hands. He will not allow your feet to be moved (Psalm 121:3), nor will He allow anything to pluck you from His hands! (John 10:28).

What an amazing King we serve! Truly, like The Shulamite confessed: *None can rival Him and there is none like Him!*

Prayer: *My Love, You are perfect in all of Your ways. You are holy and righteous, and I find no fault in You. I am so grateful today for Your perfect understanding of me. You are the one place in the whole world where I don't have to defend myself or explain my words. You know me so intimately and so perfectly. My heart finds safety in You. Today, I take my rest in Your understanding of me. I take my rest in the steadfastness of Your character. I take my rest in the restraint of Your power. Thank You for being a God of multiple chances and for loving me unconditionally through every one of those chances. None can ever rival You and, truly, there is none like You to me!*

Conversation With The King

Day Twenty-Seven
"The Favorite One"

The Bridegroom-King: *I could have chosen any from among the vast multitude of royal ones who follow Me. But unique is My beloved dove – unrivaled in beauty, without equal, beyond compare, the perfect one, the favorite one. Others see your beauty and sing of your joy. Brides and queens chant your praise: "How blessed is she!"*

- Song of Solomon 6:8-9 TPT

The King wants you to know today that you are "The Favorite One." That is your identity in Him, regardless of how you may feel or what you may have done. It's amazing how life circumstances can threaten to strip us of our identity in The King – causing us to doubt, and sometimes even forget, what He has already said about us. The Psalmist tells us in Psalm 138:2 that God magnifies His Word above His very Name. There is nothing greater than the Word of God, not even the Name of God. *Selah.* So, Beloved Shulamite, if The King magnifies His own Word above everything else, then shouldn't you do the same? What in your life right now is greater than the Name of Jesus? Nothing. So, that means nothing in your life is greater than the Word God has spoken over you and everything that concerns you. If He calls you "The Favorite One," then that is who you are!

Of all the people The King could have chosen, He chose you. The footnote for verse 8 explains that the Hebrew text for *"the vast multitude of royal ones who follow Me"* really means, *"sixty queens, eighty brides, and endless numbers of women."* Wow! You, Beloved Shulamite, are not The King's last choice – there are several others that He could have chosen. The King wants you to begin to agree with what He says about you. For too long we have agreed with what the enemy has said, what people have said, and what we have said about ourselves. But today, The King invites you into agreement with His Word. How can two truly walk together unless they are in agreement? (Amos 3:3).

Both Heaven and Hell are looking for your agreement today. Whichever kingdom you align or agree with, is the one you will find yourself walking with. If you have found that your agreement has been with the wrong kingdom, then all you have to do is break agreement with that kingdom today, repent, and ask The King to bring you back into right alignment with *His* Kingdom. He is fully devoted to you (Song of Solomon 6:3) which means He will never let you go. You are fully His and He is fully yours!

Today, The King calls you His beloved dove. He describes you as being unrivaled in beauty, without equal, and beyond compare. You are His perfect one – His favorite one. Take a moment to let the Truth of His Word sink deep into your heart. Let The Word drive out the word curses that have taken root in your heart from past seasons. Let The Word drive out the lies that have been spoken to you and about you. Let The Word drive out the condemnation, guilt, shame, and regret you've been carrying from mistakes and mess-ups. His Word is doing a deep healing work in your heart in this very moment.

> *"Is not My Word like fire," declares the Lord, "and like a hammer that breaks a rock in pieces?"*
> - Jeremiah 23:29 NIV

The King's decree over you today, Beloved Shulamite, is that people from near and far will see the beauty He sees in you, and will call you blessed! (Song of Solomon 6:9). Hear the Word of the Lord to you today and receive it by faith, in Jesus Name!

Prayer: *Sweet Dôdî, thank You for choosing me from among the vast multitude of royal ones who follow You! I feel so honored, so special, so loved. It feels so good to be chosen by You. That is my true identity: Chosen By God! Please help me to walk in that identity and to never take it for granted. Untangle my heart today from every false identity and any lie I have believed about myself. I choose to break my agreement with the kingdom of darkness and to come into full agreement with Your Word concerning me. Please help me to guard my agreement with You as I walk in this newfound identity as Your "beloved dove – unrivaled in beauty, without equal, beyond compare, the perfect one.... the favorite one!"*

Conversation With The King

Day Twenty-Eight
"Open Hearts"

The Shulamite: *I decided to go down to the valley streams where the orchards of The King grow and mature. I longed to know if hearts were opening. Are the budding vines blooming with new growth? Has their springtime of passionate love arrived?*

- Song of Solomon 6:11 TPT

For the past twenty-seven days we have examined this ongoing dialogue between The King and The Shulamite. We have reflected on the many times The Shulamite dealt with feelings of unworthiness and condemnation, and the many times The King loved her back to life despite these feelings. We have "watched" The Shulamite grow, not only in her love for The King, but also in her identity as His beloved. Beloved Shulamite, I want you to know today that every step The Shulamite has taken, you have taken with her over these twenty-seven days. The King, even in this moment, is beaming with great pleasure at your transformation and your continued desire for more of Him.

As we mature in our walk with God, the focus begins to shift from us to those around us who may not yet have a relationship with Him; or to those who once had a relationship with Him, but have strayed away. In today's reading, we see The Shulamite expressing concern for those who are in their beginning stages of walking with The King. She went down to the orchard of The King, which was the place of growth and maturity, to check on the development of "the budding vines."

I longed to know if hearts were opening.

The Shulamite was concerned about the reaction of others to The King. Were they receiving Him? Were their hearts open to Him? Were they blooming? Did they yet experience the season of passionate love? Beloved Shulamite, we are all called to evangelize and to make disciples of others (Matthew 28:19). As we grow in our own love-walk with The King, we are to be consistently mindful of those who have not yet experienced their "springtime of passionate love." The harvest is plentiful (Matthew 9:37-38) and The King is seeking willing laborers.

Where is your vineyard today? Perhaps it's your job, or home, or community, or city, or state, or country. Wherever God has you planted right now is your vineyard. Who around you needs to hear the good news about your Beloved King? The Shulamite longed to know if people's hearts were opening to The King; and our hearts, as His Beloved Shulamite, should burn daily with the same concern. The King is challenging you today to "*go down to the valley streams where His orchards grow and mature.*" Go out into the corner of the world that you currently occupy and see if the budding vines around you are blooming. The same way The King has invited you into deeper relationship with Him over these past twenty-seven days, is the same way He desires to bait others in. He calls your feet beautiful today as you run to spread the good news of His love to a dying world (Song of Solomon 7:1).

As The King's Beloved Shulamite, we know exactly where He has brought us from and all He has done to bring us to the place where we are in Him. It should, therefore, be our greatest heart's desire to bring as many "budding vines" into His orchard, for an even greater harvest. Truly, there is a harvest-sound!

Will you partner with The King in spreading the good news of the gospel today? People need to know that Jesus Christ

– our King – died, was buried, rose again from the dead, and is coming back one day for His glorious and triumphant Shulamite Bride!

Then the angel said to me, "Write these words: Wonderfully blessed are those who are invited to feast at the wedding celebration of the Lamb!" And then he said to me, "These are the true words of God."
- Revelation 19:9 TPT

Prayer: *Great King, my heart burns for the ones who have not yet come to know You as their personal Lord and Savior. I long to know if hearts are opening to You. Please make me one of Your true laborers and give me the boldness to share the gospel of Jesus Christ with everyone I meet. I hear the sound of the harvest all around me. Here I am today, Lord. Give me a fresh passion for discipleship and evangelism. Give me Your heart for the lost, the dying, and the hurting. I accept Your great commission today. I will go.*

Conversation With The King

Day Twenty-Nine
"A Claiming Love"

The Bridegroom-King: *Now I decree, I will ascend My palm tree. I will take hold of you with My power, possessing every part of My fruitful bride. Your love I will drink as wine, and your words will be Mine.*
The Shulamite: *Let us arise and run to the vineyards of Your people and see if the budding vines of love are now in full bloom. We will discover if their passion is awakened. There I will display my love for You.*
- Song of Solomon 7:8,12 TPT

The ultimate desire of The King for you is that you will allow Him to possess every part of you, so that your words will be His words. If you have been on this journey into deeper intimacy with The King then this is, no doubt, your ultimate desire as well. To know that every part of you is owned and possessed by God, and that every word you speak is in perfect alignment with His. Talk about true oneness! That is His desire for His Shulamite Bride.

Yesterday we saw The Shulamite's heart for the lost and her desire for everyone to know the depth of The King's love. Today, she continues to express her concern for the "budding vines" and invites The King to go with her to discover how far these young ones have come in their passionate desire for Him. The Shulamite longs to not just *tell* these "young ones" about The King, but to *display* her love for Him in their very presence.

The love between The Shulamite and The King was intimate, yet public. The Jerusalem-Maidens saw it and desired that same level of intimacy. The Shulamite and The King talked constantly of running away with each other to different vineyards and fields, to showcase and broadcast their love. This is your portion, Beloved Shulamite. A public love. A love that is not afraid to be seen or identified with you. This is especially significant for those who have dealt with rejection, neglect, and abandonment. For those who have felt like you were not worthy of being "claimed" or acknowledged – Beloved Shulamite, you *are* worthy of a public, claiming love!

> *You will be a beautiful crown **held high** in the hand of Yahweh, a royal crown of splendor held high in the **open palm** of your God!*
> - Isaiah 62:3 TPT

As your King claims you and publicly affirms you, be sure to make your love for Him public as well. In a world where being a Christian is met with such violent opposition and persecution, we are called to stand firm as The King's Shulamite Bride. To boldly proclaim our love and our commitment to Him, without apology or compromise. Jesus told His disciples that if they were ashamed of Him here on earth, He would be ashamed of them before His Father in Heaven (Luke 9:26). You see, The King, too, desires a public, claiming love!

How can you display your love publicly for The King today? Who can you demonstrate His love towards? (Matthew 25:40). In what ways, if any, have you been hiding your commitment to Him? How can you make a fresh commitment to Him today? Take a moment to ask The King to show you if there are areas in your life where you have wavered in demonstrating your love and commitment towards Him. Yes, our relationship with God is an individual and personal relationship, but just as our baptism was a public demonstration of our commitment to following Him – our everyday lives should continue to reflect our public, claiming love. *Selah.*

If I could only show everyone the passionate desire I have for You. If I could only express it fully, no matter who was watching me, without shame or embarrassment.
- Song of Solomon 8:1 TPT

Prayer: *King Jesus, You are my choice forever! Thank You for loving me so perfectly and so publicly. Thank You for every public display of affection and affirmation You've shown towards me. Help me to not only live out loud, but to love out loud. May others see my love for You and be led to love You too. Please strengthen me in the areas where I may have waned in my commitment. I pray for renewed zeal as I recommit my life to You today. I want You to possess every part of me, until people identify me as Yours.*

Conversation With The King

Day Thirty
"Unrelenting Fire"

The Bridegroom-King: *Who is this one? She arises out of her desert, clinging to her Beloved.... Fasten Me upon your heart as a seal of fire forevermore. This living, consuming flame will seal you as My prisoner of love... Place this fierce, unrelenting fire over your entire being.*
- Song of Solomon 8:5-6 TPT

The world is just now beginning to come out of what has felt like a long, wilderness season. Many have lost loved ones, jobs, relationships, and *hope* – the sense of global heaviness has indeed been great. You may find yourself today wondering where to go from here, or how to pick yourself up from this place and move forward. But, be encouraged that The King has already scheduled your exodus from this desert season.

    When we talk about being in desert or wilderness seasons, what's usually implied is a feeling of barrenness, isolation, fruitlessness, lack, or hopelessness. Desert-like seasons are often times of transition, testing, and training. As we consider The King speaking of The Shulamite in today's reading, He describes her as *emerging* from the desert – that dry and barren place – *leaning* on the shoulder of the One she loves. He is helping her up, out of this low place. Beloved Shulamite, this is a reflection of us as The King's Shulamite Bride – The Church – coming up from the desert, leaning on the everlasting arms of our Beloved King!

    Notice that The Shulamite did not emerge from the desert on her own. The fact that she was leaning on her Beloved implies that she was weak, exhausted, and could not carry herself. Perhaps that's where you are today. Exhausted and powerless. If that is how you feel, Beloved Shulamite, know that The King is with you even in your desert place; and He is ready to help you up and lead you out. How did you make it through 2020? Leaning on your Beloved! How are you going to make it through 2021 and beyond? Leaning on your Beloved!

To lean means to rest against something; to bend; or to cast one's weight to one side for support. The King invites you today to cast your weight – your cares – on Him. You won't be able to come up from the desert if you're fighting to stand up straight, or trying to do it in your own strength. The King beckons you to lean back into His arms today so He can carry you.

Once securely in The King's arms, He instructs The Shulamite to *fasten Him upon her heart as a seal*. That speaks to being so closely knitted together that there is no room for anything or anyone to come between. The Shulamite is forever marked by the King's seal on her heart. Beloved Shulamite, as your King carries you in this season, choose to cling so tightly to Him that your hearts beat in synchrony. That you inhale His exhale. That your gaze gets lost in His eyes. That is the level of closeness The King desires to have with you.

He calls The Shulamite – as He calls you today – His *prisoner of love*. Imagine being held captive by The King's unrelenting fire of love! What a picture of The Lord, Most Passionate! The Shulamite is so consumed as He charges her to *place His love all over her entire being*. This is so important because it's one thing to know God loves you, but it's an entirely different experience to actually internalize and live from that love.

Beloved Shulamite, as you lean on your King in this season, He wants to lead you *out* of the desert and *into* the prison of His love, where every part of your being is consumed by His fierce, unrelenting fire. There is no safer or more secure place in the entire universe. Will you lean back today?

Prayer: *O God, Most Passionate! Make me Your prisoner of love today as I fasten You to my heart. Mark me with Your seal and consume me with Your fierce, unrelenting fire. I choose to lean back into Your arms in the midst of my desert-like season. I have tried to do it on my own, but I'm too weak and exhausted to carry myself. Will You carry me, my Beloved? It has been a trying season and I desire nothing more than to rest in the safety of Your everlasting arms. I place Your fiery love all over my being today – I internalize and come into full agreement with Your unrelenting love for me. From this day forward, may I live into the God-given identity of, "Fiercely Loved."*

Conversation With The King

Day Thirty-One
"Unquenchable Love"

The Bridegroom-King: *Rivers of pain and persecution will never extinguish this flame. Endless floods will be unable to quench this raging fire that burns within you. Everything will be consumed. It will stop at nothing as you yield everything to this furious fire, until it won't even seem to you like a sacrifice anymore.*
- Song of Solomon 8:7 TPT

On this Thirty-First Day of Intimacy with The King, He wants to thoroughly convince you of His passion and unquenchable love for you. In yesterday's reading, The King invited The Shulamite to *place His unrelenting fire of love over her entire being* – to subsume His love with her whole mind, will, emotions, and strength. He continues to describe His love today as *unextinguishable*. Beloved Shulamite, there is nothing that you are facing, have faced, or will ever face in this life that will douse the flame of The King's unrelenting, unquenchable love for you. Let that Truth settle your heart and settle every matter in your life today.

The King begins to describe the various things that may try to oppose His love for The Shulamite – *floods*, *pain*, and *persecution* – but, assures her that not even these threats can quench the flame of His love that burns deep in her soul. Know today that it is impossible for *any* life circumstance to overwhelm God's love *for* you and *in* you. That's why He tells you to place His love all over your being. To let no area of your life be uncovered or unsoaked by the fire of His love.

Many waters cannot quench love.

Regardless of where you find yourself today, or the magnitude of the situation you may be facing, The King wants you to know that His love for you cannot be overpowered, diminished, or even *controlled*. No one can *control* God's love for you. That's a powerful Truth if you've been held captive by "the overseers," or judgmental, self-appointed prison wardens. The King's love cannot be manipulated or influenced by human opinion or any form of condemnation. The King works all things according to the counsel of His own will (Ephesians 1:11), which means He takes His *own* counsel concerning you. Beloved Shulamite, your King does not confer with man concerning any plan He has for your life. None of the purposes He has ordained for you will be withheld from Him (Job 42:2), regardless of the floods, persecution, or pain you've endured.

Whatever your "many waters" is today, know that you are unconditionally and unrelentingly loved; and as you yield day-by-day to The King's love, *everything* in your life will be consumed. No sacrifice will seem too great as you willingly submit to this fire. It is the fire of His love that purges, purifies, refines, molds, heals, and restores. It may not always feel comfortable – remember *myrrh* is one of The King's spices – but if you surrender to His fiery passion, you will emerge as pure gold! (Job 23:10).

Pure gold has always been how The King sees you; and every day of your life has been an invitation into seeing yourself in the same light. Every trial or test you have faced has been divinely orchestrated to illuminate your shine. Life has not been working against you, but it has been working *for* you far more than you realize. Beloved Shulamite, commit today to allowing The King's unquenchable fire to set you ablaze. Yield to its refining heat. Let it burn away the chaff. Allow The King's fiery love into the closed-off spaces of your heart. Then prepare to be blinded by the radiance of His reflection in and through you! *Here's to a golden life!*

Prayer: *O King of Glory! My Beloved! My Refiner! Lover of my Soul! I love and adore You today with my whole heart. Thank You for Your relentless and unquenchable love for me. Thank You for the all-consuming fire of Your love and all that it is accomplishing in me even now. I yield completely to the fire of Your love! Cause me to shine in pure radiance before You. May people see the light in me and be led to glorify You. Thank You for pouring into me over these Thirty-One Days of Intimacy. Help me to continue the conversation with You as Your Shulamite. My heart and soul long for more and more of You. Here I am, Lord. I give you a limitless and uninhibited "Yes!" for the rest of my life! I am forever Yours.*

Conversation With The King

The Bridegroom And The Bride In Divine Duet

The Bridegroom-King: *Arise, My darling!*
The Shulamite: *Come quickly, my Beloved.*
The Bridegroom-King: *Come and be the graceful gazelle with Me.*
The Shulamite: *Come be like a young stag with me.*
The Bridegroom-King: *We will dance in the High Place of the sky,*
The Shulamite: *Yes, on the mountains of fragrant spice.*
The Bridegroom-King: *Forever we shall be united as one!*
- Song of Solomon 8:14 TPT

Beloved Shulamite, I could not end this *Conversation Between The Shulamite and The King* without making mention of that glorious day when we will dance with our Bridegroom-King *"on the mountains of fragrant spice."* Myrrh is one of The King's fragrant spices – a spice of suffering, bitterness, and pain. But, one day we will dance together with Him ON the myrrh! ON the very things and situations that caused us pain, grief, and bitterness in this life. Glory to God!

This, Beloved Shulamite, is the true essence of The King *"turning our mourning into dancing"* (Psalm 30:11). What a day that will be when the bitter is turned into sweet, when all our tears are wiped away (Revelation 21:4), and we are forever united as one – in complete divine bliss – with our Beloved Bridegroom-King! I cannot wait for that glorious day!

Maranatha!

Prayer From Ephesians 3:16-19 TPT

As we have come to the end of our Thirty-One Days of Intimacy – and as you continue on your own journey with The King – I'd like to pray Ephesians 3:16-19 TPT over you:

I pray that [The King] would unveil within you the unlimited riches of His glory and favor, until supernatural strength floods your innermost being with His divine might and explosive power. Then, by constantly using your faith, the life of Christ will be released deep inside you, and the resting place of [The King's] love will become the very Source and Root of your life. Then, you will be empowered to discover what every holy one experiences – the great magnitude of the astonishing love of Christ in all its dimensions. How deeply intimate and far-reaching is His love! How enduring and inclusive it is! Endless love beyond measurement that transcends our understanding – [may] this extravagant love pour into you, until you are filled to overflowing with the fullness of God! Amen.

Reference

Asbury, C. (2018). Reckless Love. On *Reckless Love*. Bethel Music.
https://www.youtube.com/watch?v=6xx0d3R2LoU

About The Author

Dr. Neisha-Ann Thompson is a prophetic intercessor, professional psychologist, speaker, and author of several books. She is the Founder and Host of *The Midnight Cry Prayer Call*, a global prayer ministry with subscribers across three continents. She is a registered Thorough-Format Minister with *Restoring The Foundations* and has a heart for healing and deliverance.

With a doctorate in counseling psychology, a heart for ministry, and a passion for God's Word, she adopts a psychospiritual teaching approach to help people discover their spiritual identity and purpose in God, and practically apply the Word of God to their lives.

Connect with her at **www.neisha-annthompson.com**.

For previous *Midnight Cry Prayer Call* recordings:
Visit **youtube.com/c/mncprayercall**.

Made in the USA
Middletown, DE
18 September 2021